ONCE-BORN, TWICE-BORN ZEN:
The Soto and Rinzai Schools
of Japanese Zen

ONCE-BORN, TWICE-BORN ZEN
The Soto and Rinzai Schools of Japanese Zen

by Conrad Hyers

Longwood Academic
Wolfeboro, New Hampshire

Published in 1989 by Longwood Academic, a division of
Longwood Publishing Group, Inc., Wolfeboro, N.H.,
03894-2069, U.S.A.

ISBN 0-89341-523-5 (cloth)
      0-89341-524-3 (paperback)

Printed in the United States of America.

Library of Congress Cataloging in Publication Data:

Hyers, M. Conrad
  Once-born, twice-born Zen
  Bibliography: p.
  Includes index.
  1. Zen Buddhism—Japan. 2. Sotoshu. 3. Rinzai
(Sect) I. Title.
BQ9262.9.J3H94 1989   294.3'927   88-13789
ISBN 0-89341-523-5
ISBN 0-89341-524-3 (pbk.)

In remembrance of the kindnesses of

OGATA SOHAKU
and
DOI MASATOSHI

ACKNOWLEDGMENTS

Preliminary sketches of the materials that form this book were initially presented as papers to the American Academy of Religion in San Francisco, to the Congress of the International Association for the History of Religions in Winnipeg, Canada, and to the International Symposium on Reversal Theory at the University of Cardiff, Wales. Programmatic essays were subsequently selected for publication in books developed from the latter two conferences: *Traditions in Contact and Change, Selected Proceedings from the XIVth Congress of the International Association for the History of Religions,* edited by Peter Slater and Donald Wiebe (Waterloo, Ontario: Wilfrid Laurier University Press, 1983), © 1983 Canadian Corporation for Studies in Religion; and *Reversal Theory: Applications and Developments,* edited by M.J. Apter, D. Fontana, and S. Murgatroyd (Cardiff, Wales: University College Cardiff Press, 1985), © 1985 University College Cardiff. Grateful acknowledgment is given to these editors and publishers for permission to use, in considerably expanded and revised form, materials which originally appeared in these contexts.

Acknowledgment is also made for materials drawn from the following sources:

To Columbia University Press for excerpts from Philip Yampolsky, *The Zen Master Hakuin: Selected Writings,* copyright © 1971 Columbia University Press. Used by permission.

To Doubleday and Company for an excerpt from *An Introduction to Haiku,* translated by Harold G. Henderson. Copyright © 1978, 1979 by Zen Center, Inc. Reprinted by permission of Doubleday, a division of Bantam, Doubleday, Dell Publishing Group, Inc.

To Doubleday and Company for excerpts from *Three Pillars of Zen* by Philip Kapleau. Copyright © 1965 by Philip Kapleau. Copyright © 1980 by Doubleday, a division of Bantam, Doubleday, Dell Publishing Group, Inc. Reprinted by permission of the publisher.

To John Weatherhill Inc. for excerpts from *Zen Mind, Beginner's Mind* by Shunryu Suzuki, edited by Trudy Dixon, with a preface by Huston Smith and an introduction by Richard Baker. Copyright © 1970 by John Weatherhill Inc. Permission applied for.

To Nakayama Shobo for excerpts from Dogen Zenji's *Shobogenzo,* translated by Kosen Nishiyama and John Stevens, Vol. II Copyright © 1977 by Kosen Nishiyama and John Stevens. Permission applied for.

To Shambala Publications for excerpts from *Dogen's Formative Years in China* by Takashi James Kodera © 1980. Reprinted by arrangement with Shambala Publications, Inc., 300 Massachusetts Avenue, Boston, MA 02115.

To The University of Arizona Press for excerpts from *Dogen Kigen, Mystical Realist* by Hee-jin Kim. Copyright © 1975 by The University of Arizona Press. Used by permission.

Acknowledgement is also gratefully given for the use of the portraits of Dogen and Hakuin in the frontispiece. The portrait of Dogen is from *Dogen's Formative Years in China* by Takashi James Kodera, (Boulder: Prajna Press, 1980). Acknowledgement is given to a frontispiece in *Dogen to sono deshi* (Tokyo: Mainichi Shimbun-sha, 1972). The self-portrait of Hakuin Zenji is from a private printing of a book in Kyoto, 1967.

CONTENTS

Portrait of Dogen, in the possession
of the Hokyo-ji in Fukui Prefecture

Hakuin Zenji
Self-portrait

PROLOGUE

The Zen Mystique

During a public reading at St. Louis University by Lucien Stryk from his translation of *After Images: Zen Poems of Shinkichi Takahashi*, the following incident occurred. A young woman in the audience took a copy of the book from which he was reading (and which she had purchased on entering the hall) and began tearing it up into small pieces. Stryk had just finished some introductory remarks on the nature of Zen and was beginning to read the Zen poems. The noise of the disturbance was such that some in the audience began to complain that they could not hear. The woman replied, "I know," and kept on tearing pages. Stryk kept on reading. As the atmosphere became tense, someone interrupted to say that the tearing was probably an attempt to communicate something in a Zen fashion. Stryk replied that he had received the message, and continued reading.

When the book was in shreds, another woman picked up the pieces, carried them to the front of the hall, and laid them like an offering at Stryk's feet. She then gasshoed and Stryk gasshoed in return, saying the word *gassho* out loud as he did so. The two women proceeded to leave and made their way with some difficulty out of the crowded hall. Stryk continued to read the Zen poems. But, after a time, because the tension was mounting in the room, Stryk stopped his reading and commented that, as he was not a Zen master, he would not attempt to pass judgment on the actions of the women, except to say that the commotion they created in the process "gave them away by their awkwardness."

1

The women, it turned out, were instructors in Oriental Philosophy and saw themselves as students of Rinzai Zen. The actions, they later said, were not premeditated, nor motivated by any particular hostility to Stryk. They were "spontaneous gestures," and at the time they had immediately known just what they must do. The one woman said that her presentation of the torn pages had been a moment of potential enlightenment for Stryk, but that he had resisted the opportunity, as evidenced by his nervous and unnecessary pronunciation of the word *gassho* as he bowed.

The woman who had destroyed the book indicated that, on three occasions in the past, she had burned her entire library of Zen books, and that on this occasion the paradox of lecturing on Zen had again overwhelmed her. Zen, she insisted, is the "wordless dharma," the unteachable teaching, and any attempt at putting it into words is futile and self-contradictory. An interviewer offered her a copy of the book by Lucien Stryk, which she accepted!

The Mystification of Zen

Zen Buddhism in the recent decades of its popularity in the West, particularly during the "flower/pot" era of the Sixties and Seventies, has commonly been presented as thoroughly enigmatic in character. No matter that great Zen masters themselves had lectured, preached, admonished, and written—in words, of course. No matter that Buddhism is in possession of a considerable scripture in the Pali Canon alone, as well as the vast Mahayana corpus. No matter that certain Mahayana sutras, such as the *Prajnaparamita,* the *Avatamsaka,* the *Vajracheddika,* the *Vimalakirti,* and the *Lankavatara* were favored by early Chinese masters. No matter that various sutras are chanted daily in Zen monasteries. No matter that the greatest of Japanese masters, Dogen and Hakuin, both wrote vigorously and voluminously. What was of paramount interest was Zen wordlessness and the Zen debunking of words. That theme conformed with the subjectivism and anti-authoritarianism of the time.

Collections of obscure anecdotes and nonsensical koans tantalized Occidental imaginations schooled in Aristotelian logic, Cartesian philosophy, and Newtonian thinking. Images of Zen masters tearing up sutra scrolls, insulting buddhas and patriarchs, shouting and kicking disciples, putting sandals on their heads, juggling with wooden balls, holding up fly-whisks in silence, or defying the laws of non-contradiction and excluded middle whenever they pleased, provided a new type of hero for the growing cult of anti-intellectualism. The further association of Zen with spontaneity and immediacy—however removed that might be from the actual rigor and regimentation of monastic life and meditational practice—offered welcome support to those seeking instant emancipation from law and order, regulations, personal discipline, the establishment, and piano lessons. And the promise of some sudden, earth-shaking, mind-boggling experience of enlightenment had special psychedelic appeal to those otherwise seeking instant mystical highs and alternative states of consciousness.

In such a context Zen was easily construed as being fundamentally impervious to rational thought or intelligible interpretation. Zen was the quintessential product of the inscrutable Oriental mind, cloaked in the ineffability of mysticism in general and Buddhist enlightenment in particular, and cloistered behind esoteric monastic walls in a distant and exotic land. Though books proliferated on the subject, and courses on Asian mysticism began invading college and university catalogs, and the lecture tour gave the matter its own brand of Chautauqua coverage, it was nonetheless insisted upon that Zen was not something that properly could be discussed, written about, lectured on, or other-wise elucidated by means of psychology, philosophy, history, sociology, or any other tools of Western intellectualism. Every attempt at interpreting Zen, let alone explaining it, needed to be accompanied by a disclaimer that, of course and unfortunately, nothing could be said about it. Zen represented the destruction of all explanations, the collapsing of all interpretive categories of the mind, as a prelude to transcending all words, concepts, and discriminations in an epiphany of silence.

Though there is an important truth in all of this, to which I have paid tribute in my *Zen and the Comic Spirit*,[1] like most truths it is not the whole of the truth. No experience—even the experience of basking in the sun or eating a banana—can be completely arrived at, captured, comprehended, or exhausted by words. But it does not follow that words are completely irrelevant, or irredeemably distorting, or incapable of elucidating experience at all. Words present a great many problems, to be sure, but words are a specifically and

3

wondrously human occupation. To reduce words to the world of maya is to miss the extent to which they are a distinctive human gift and achievement. In and through words the truth is revealed and hidden at the same time. That is the paradox of words. Words are "the finger pointing at the moon"—to use an ancient Buddhist simile—and, as such, should not be confused with the moon. Yet they are still capable of pointing in the general direction. Must the rational mind and the intuitive mind always quarrel about this?

> *On how to sing*
> *The frog school and the skylark school*
> *Are arguing.*
>
> Shiki[2]

In the West the attempt to present and preserve authentic Zen has often led to inauthentic conclusions. In the name of protecting the fundamental experiences and insights of Zen the result has been to mystify Zen, throwing a dust-cloud of obscurantism around a tradition which, ironically, concerns itself with seeing more clearly and directly. The great Soto Zen master of the 13th century, Dogen, offered a more balanced view. On the one hand, wrote Dogen, "Nothing can be gained by extensive study and wide reading. . . . Writing prose and poetry is, in the long run, useless; thus, it should be given up . . . . Be sure to keep away from the scriptural teachings of the sects of esoteric and exoteric Buddhism. Even the *Records* of the Zen Patriarchs should not be studied on too wide a scale."[3]

On the other hand, Dogen lectured, preached, and wrote a good deal about Zen for the benefit of his disciples and others. He did not subscribe exclusively to the so-called Zen creed: "Special transmission outside the scriptures, direct-pointing to the heart of man, looking into one's own nature." Dogen objected to the distinction between external and internal knowledge: the dharma contained in the Buddhist sutras and the dharma transmitted from master to disciple. For him there was only one dharma which is transmitted through both. "To believe that there is a special transmission outside the scriptures is to misinterpret the Buddhist teaching."[4]

Dogen likewise rejected the Zen tradition which argues that the Buddha transmitted anything to Kasyapa (the first in the line of Zen patriarchs) that was separate from or other than the teachings of the

Buddhist sutras. There is only one Buddhist dharma, in whatever form it may be expressed. Dogen cited favorably the response of Haryo to a monk's question as to whether the spirit of the Patriarchs and the spirit of the sutras were the same or different: "When a chicken is cold it climbs a tree; when a duck is cold it goes into the water."[5]

In the legend of the Buddha's transmission of Zen to Kasyapa, when the Buddha summarizes the essence of his teaching by holding up a sandalwood flower and Kasyapa smiles in response, the Buddha then says, "I possess the Eye and Treasury of the True Law and the Serene Mind of Nirvana. I now bestow it on Mahakasyapa." Concerning the common interpretation of this as a secret, wordless teaching, preserved in its purity by the Zen tradition, Dogen remarks: "If Shakyamuni disliked words and liked to hold up flowers, then these words should have preceded the holding up of the flower!"[6]

To some extent the differing emphases of Rinzai and Soto Zen are already visible in this issue of words and the transmission of the dharma. It was *Rinzai* Zen that was presented as offering a revolutionary experience and insight capable of shattering all categories of thought, sweeping away all "academic exercises," and turning the world upside down. It was *Rinzai* Zen that bewildered Western minds, accustomed to rational argument and empirical demonstration, with the koan whose enigmatic or contradictory or nonsensical character made intellectual understanding impossible, brought inner and outer tensions to a head, and promised to burst the bonds of ignorance, like a time bomb ticking in the depths of consciousness.

This was *not* the Zen of the Soto school and its greatest exponent, Dogen, who made little use of the koan, extreme techniques, or devices aimed at increasing tension, frustration, doubt, and despair in the hope of precipitating a sudden experience of insight. The woman who tore up Lucien Stryk's book during a public reading was behaving in accord with many a Zen anecdote favored by Rinzai teaching. The torn pages were presented to Stryk while he read Zen poems, as if this were a kind of koan ("the paradox of lecturing on Zen") and "a moment of potential enlightenment" for Stryk. Whether or not the woman—who said she was a student of Rinzai Zen—properly or accurately represented the Rinzai tradition in that context, the anecdote raises the question of the differences between types of Zen and their respective techniques and understandings. Rinzai is not the whole of the Zen world, nor is it the only form of Zen experience.

CHAPTER I

The Varieties of Zen Experience

Western literature on Zen has tended to present Zen as a relatively homogeneous experience and teaching, a kind of seamless garment of truth. If this picture of uniformity were true it would indeed be remarkable, considering that Zen has existed in many traditions or schools over the past 1200 years of documentable history, and has had not only Chinese and Japanese but Korean and Vietnamese forms. Zen is, in fact, noted for being blessed with an array of masters who are hardly anonymous clones of their predecessors but who have the reputation of being strong, singular personalities whose Zen teaching and practice has a distinctive flavor of its own from one master to another.

Beyond the fact that Zen in its literal sense of "meditation" is found in some form and degree of importance in many types of Buddhism, and for that matter in any of the schools of yoga that developed in India, there is still considerable variety within that one small stream of meditation practice that traces its lineage to Indian Buddhism through the shadowy figure of Bodhidharma, who crossed the seas to China in the 6th century A.D. The myth of the monolithic Zen experience, teaching, or practice has no substance either in its Chinese setting or later Korean, Japanese, and Vietnamese forms.

The anecdotes concerning Bodhidharma are themselves sufficiently sketchy and legendary to permit several lines of interpretation as to what it was he brought, taught, and otherwise transmitted from India to China. Clearest is his emphasis upon meditation (Sanskrit, *dhyana;* Chinese, *ch'an;* Japanese, *zen*). Hence

7

those who have followed in this emphasis came to be referred to as the Meditation School. Exactly what he meant by meditation, however, is not clear, as well as what he saw as its techniques and objectives. Also unclear are the similarities and differences between Bodhidharma-zen and other forms of Indian *dhyana*—a common term in yoga systems—or its relationship to monastic rule (*vinaya*), Buddhist scripture (*sutra*), and the teaching of doctrine (*dharma*).

After Bodhidharma, different masters became focal points of different strains of meditation-teaching, standing in different relationships to Bodhidharma, Chinese Taoism, and other forms of Chinese Buddhism. For several centuries Zen (Ch'an) appears to have been a very fluid tradition, with schools developing along various lines of teaching, practice and application, and not without their "bones of contention." Quite early, too, a major rift developed between the Northern "gradual enlightenment" and the Southern "sudden enlightenment" schools. The Southern branch was in turn to become at least five major schools, the "five mountains" of Zen. And two of these schools became the basis in the 13th century for the two major sects of Japanese Zen, Rinzai and Soto, which differ in several important ways. Japanese tradition has it, in fact, that there were twenty-four schools introduced to Japan from China, either by Chinese monks coming to Japan or by Japanese monks returning from China. One of these, surviving in small numbers in the Kyoto area, is Obaku Zen, which makes meditational use of the Pure Land chant of the *nembutsu* (*namu amida butsu,* "praise to the Amida Buddha").

The Domination of Rinzai

Part of the monolithic image of Zen in the West is the result of the fact that, prior to 1970, almost all of the literature in English on Zen was derived from the Rinzai school. This is also, as has been noted, one reason for the mystification of Zen that prevailed during the same period, since it is the Rinzai school which places considerable emphasis upon the meditational use of koans and such non-verbal devices as shouting, kicking, and striking. It is in Rinzai that so much attention is devoted to breaking down the intellectual attempt at appropriating truth through words and concepts, crushing the illusory ego and its grasping, and collapsing the separations of the subject/object split. The resolute intent of Rinzai Zen is to destroy the false

8

ways of thinking and responding which make up the maya of ordinary consciousness, and to bring about a revolution in consciousness through which one is able to see immediately and clearly out of the purity of one's true self.

Perhaps the popularity of Zen during the tumultuous period of the Sixties and early Seventies was in part because it *was* Rinzai Zen, appearing as it did—incorrectly, by and large—to be so easily accommodated to the spirit of the times with its anti-intellectualism and anti-legalism, its desire for immediate and intuitive experience, its searching for altered states of consciousness, and its general interest in breaking things down, tearing up the fabric of society, and revolutionizing commonly accepted patterns. Rinzai literature was replete with testimonials of dramatic, ecstatic experiences that had overwhelmed and transformed people's lives. "It was as though I had taken one small step and the whole universe turned inside out," writes one respondent.[1] Another reports: "There was no before and after. Everything was as though suspended. The object of my own meditation and my own self had disappeared. The only thing I felt was that my own innermost self was completely united and filled with everything above and below and all around."[2]

Much of the early literature on Zen was by the Rinzai scholar Daisetz T. Suzuki, who dominated the field for half a century with twenty books and frequent articles in English. Founder of *The Eastern Buddhist* in 1910 and author of his first collection of *Essays in Zen Buddhism* in English in 1927, D.T. Suzuki taught, wrote, and lectured on Zen and Mahayana Buddhism until his death in 1966 at the age of 95. Zen in the West was largely Suzuki Zen. And Suzuki Zen was Rinzai Zen.

Certain Rinzai masters, too, such as Shohaku Ogata and Shibayama-roshi, had works published in English. Films on Zen, such as Ruth Stephan's *Zen in Ryoko-in*, featured life and practice in the Rinzai tradition. Inevitably most Western writers on the subject based their work entirely on Rinzai Zen, if not Suzuki Zen. This bias was further reinforced by the fact that much of the Zen literature translated consisted of collections of koans, favored by Rinzai Zen, such as the *Mumonkan* and *Hekiganroku*, and anecdotal records of Zen monks being suddenly enlightened after having been kicked in the chest, deafened by the master's shout, struck on the head with a roof tile,

9

and the like. Zen practice and experience equaled Rinzai practice and experience, as in Heinrich Dumoulin's description of the fundamental concern of Zen, which is stated in classical Rinzai terms: "Man must undergo a conversion, a breakthrough or awakening, in order to become his true self and gain access to what is authentically real. Zen Buddhism names this conversion the 'great death'—the sole way by which man can enter true life."[3] There is no acknowledgement and apparently no recognition that, of the two major Zen sects in Japan, this is the specifically Rinzai way of putting it.

Only in the last two decades has a literature begun to develop in English out of the Soto sect (ironically, much the larger of the two in Japan) with the work of emigrated Soto masters such as Shunryu Suzuki and Taizan Maezumi,[4] their Western disciples, and Zen scholars such as Masao Abe. This has been aided further by the efforts of various people at translating the definitive Soto classic, Dogen's voluminous *Shobogenzo*.[5] The world of Japanese Soto, and especially that of its founding father and philosophical genius Dogen, is now becoming sufficiently well-known in the West to be no longer avoidable or reducible to Rinzai Zen. Still, the major differences between the two schools and their interpretations of Zen practice and its implications are not well understood or appreciated. Such is the special concern of this book.

The Two Suzukis

In his preface to Soto master Shunryu Suzuki's book *Zen Mind, Beginner's Mind* (1970), Huston Smith noted the marked difference between the two Suzukis and their contrasting emphases. "Whereas Daisetz Suzuki's Zen was dramatic, Shunryu Suzuki's is ordinary. *Satori* (enlightenment) was focal for Daisetz, and it was in large part the fascination of this extraordinary state that made his writings so compelling. In Shunryu Suzuki's book the words *satori* and *kensho*, its near-equivalent, never appear."[6] The observation is quite telling. Rinzai Zen aims at precipitating an ecstatic experience of enlightenment through such devices as unrelenting concentration on one's koan and frequent *dokusan* (interview) sessions with the master in which one's koan-concentration is encouraged, questioned, and tested. Soto Zen stresses enlightenment as the center of one's being and life; it is not a goal to strive after but an ever-present reality, and not attainable because it is the basis of all attainment.

Though it is incorrect to say that the words *satori* ("insight") and *kensho* ("seeing into one's own nature") do not appear in Shunryu Suzuki's teaching, or that of Soto generally, they are given a different context and value. The Rinzai emphasis upon struggling with a koan toward a sudden experience of insight and a dramatic revolution in consciousness is not characteristic of Soto. When Huston Smith had occasion to interview Shunryu Suzuki shortly before his death, he asked why satori wasn't stressed in his book. The roshi's wife leaned over and whispered playfully, "It's because he hasn't had one!" The roshi batted her with his fan, and with equally playful worriment on his face put his finger to his lips, saying, "Shhh! Don't tell him."[7]

It is not just that Soto de-emphasizes the experience of satori—though it does—but that it reinterprets the matter in a significantly different way. Soto also gives a much smaller value to dramatic experiences in general, as their very character is seen as inconsistent with the equanimity and tranquillity of the Buddha-nature. Extreme emotional experiences cannot in themselves represent enlightenment or true understanding, for the Buddha-nature is calm and undisturbed. Emotional highs—and the lows that precede and often follow them—are part of the manic/depressive syndrome which is hardly characteristic of the Buddhist state of emptiness (*sunyata*). If emotional highs and abrupt realizations occur, one should not dwell on them or be enticed by them. "Enlightenment," Shunryu Suzuki taught, "is not some good feeling or some particular state of mind. The state of mind that exists when you sit in the right posture is, itself, enlightenment. If you cannot be satisfied with the state of mind you have in zazen, it means your mind is still wandering about. . . In this posture there is no need to talk about the right state of mind. You already have it. This is the conclusion of Buddhism."[8] Or again, "The Zen school is based on our actual nature, on our true mind as expressed and realized in practice. . . . We practice zazen to express our true nature, not to attain enlightenment. Bodhidharma's Buddhism is to *be* practice, to *be* enlightenment."[9]

While it is true that Soto masters have been known to make some use of koans and abrupt-teaching methods, and Rinzai masters have been known to make some use of zazen-only without making it focus on a koan, still there are important differences between the schools

11

that are not reducible to a matter of emphasis or degree. Some masters, also, have started in one tradition and, unable to find a suitable teacher, or otherwise dissatisfied, have taken up practice in the other tradition. Daiun Harada-roshi and his disciple Hakuun Yasutani-roshi are cases in point, both having moved from Soto to Rinzai practice, and both having attempted to draw upon both traditions in their teaching. They became and remained basically Rinzai, however, and at critical points interpreted issues from a Rinzai standpoint, accommodating Soto to that.[10]

Granting that the heart of Zen is *zen* (meditation), the issue is still what kind of zen preoccupies the Rinzai and Soto schools respectively, and the reasons for these preoccupations. What are the differences between the techniques of Rinzai and Soto, and the experiences fostered by these techniques? And what are the implications of these differences? On the other hand, despite these various differences, to what extent do the Rinzai and Soto schools nevertheless form a unity? In this and subsequent chapters we will proceed by sharpening the differences, and will attempt to understand the reasons for these differences and their significance. The final chapters will discuss the underlying unities of these contrasting forms of Zen, as well as the uniqueness of their respective contributions to Buddhist self-understanding.

Some Preliminary Contrasts

Rinzai sees zen practice primarily in terms of koan-zen, an intense concentration of one's whole being upon a koan, with the intent of breaking down the hold of the ego, frustrating desire and attachment, and confounding the ordinary ''discriminating mind.'' Soto makes little use of the koan, placing major emphasis upon *zazen* (sitting meditation) or, as it is also called in contrast to koan-meditation, *shikantaza* (just sitting). Here one does not meditate or concentrate the mind upon anything, whether Buddhist precept, life of the Buddha, image of a Bodhisattva, mantric formula, or mandala, let alone koan. As the Chinese Soto master Ju-ching phrased it: ''This is the single-minded intense sitting without burning incense, worshipping, reciting the *nembutsu*, doing penance, or chanting sutras.''[11]

Rinzai stresses the false and illusory ways of thinking and being from which one must be awakened and liberated through the power of koan-concentration. In order to make great spiritual strides, one must have, or have developed, a profound sense of disquiet, if not despair, concerning one's illusory state of ego, desire, and attachment. Roshi Philip Kapleau, one of the major American advocates of Rinzai Zen, writes: "If you study the cases of those who have truly and deeply awakened, you will find that in virtually every case the awakening came after much soul-searching, prompted either by a gnawing dissatisfaction with one's life or by personal anguish growing out of a traumatic emotional experience." Thus he goes on to argue that the central aim of Zen practice is either to bring to a crisis-point a pre-existing state of disquietude or to precipitate it. "Formal Zen training is basically nothing more than the master's effort to stimulate this intense questioning, this doubt-mass, when it does not arise spontaneously."[13]

For Rinzai, meditation is a form of the profoundest questioning, a fundamental quandary brought into painfully sharpened focus by the relentless pressure of the koan and attendant practices such as shouting and striking. It is a bringing of the deepest doubts and anxieties to a breaking point by concentrating them in the koan, where their collective energies are compressed to the point that a resolution finally bursts forth—or the individual goes mad. As D.T. Suzuki describes the relation between koan and meditation: " *Dhyana* or *zazen* is used as the means of reaching the solution of the *koan*. Zen does not make *dhyana* an end in itself, for apart from the *koan* exercise, the practicing of *zazen* is a secondary consideration. . . . *Koan* and *zazen* are the two handmaids of Zen, the first is the eye and the second is the foot."[14]

In Soto Zen, however, zazen *is* an end-in-itself, not a means to some other end. It is the enjoyment of one's intrinsic Buddha-nature. Soto stresses sitting within one's enlightened Buddha-nature, allowing this original Buddha-mind to well up and flow through all areas of one's consciousness and life. One does not begin by building up a strong sense of false and illusory ways of thinking and being, but a positive sense of fundamental well-being which can neither be created nor destroyed, lost or achieved. Thus Shunryu Suzuki says, "It is not after we practice zazen that we realize the truth; even before we practice zazen, realization is there. It is not after we understand the truth that we attain enlightenment. . . . This is Bodhidharma's zazen: Even before we practice it, enlightenment is there."[15]

In Soto zazen is also hardly the "foot" of the Zen way, as D.T. Suzuki suggests, running or even trudging toward the distant finish line of Buddhism. Zazen is not even the eye of Zen, as D.T. Suzuki claims of the koan. It is the act of sitting at the center of one's being, and of all being, where there is no distinction between eye and foot, means and goal, self and other. Again Shunryu Suzuki comments: "The most important thing is to forget all gaining ideas, all dualistic thoughts. . . . Just practice zazen in a certain posture. Do not think about anything. Just remain on your cushion without expecting anything. Then eventually you will resume your own true nature. That is to say, your own true nature resumes itself."[16]

For Soto Zen, sitting in meditation is the most natural, comfortable, simple, original way to sit. Rather than a life-and-death struggle with a koan which aims to bring inner conflicts and crises to a fever pitch, or in their apparent absence to foster them, in Soto meditation one sits in a calm faith in one's inherent Buddha-nature. Like a camel sitting by an oasis in the midst of the surrounding desert, the Soto practitioner sits at the harmonious center of individual and collective being, where one is refreshed and renewed at the wellspring of consciousness.

Thus, whereas Rinzai talks about having an abruptly transforming experience of satori/kensho in which the illusions and delusions of maya/avidya are broken through, Soto talks about the "nothing special," ordinary, everyday experiences wherein one draws upon the resources of one's Buddha-nature which is already enlightened, already free, already at peace. While Rinzai tends to be conflict and crisis-oriented, cultivating doubt and aiming at a defeat of the enemy within in order to achieve a radical reconstitution of the psyche, Soto speaks of faith in an underlying harmony and unity within which one is invited to sit naturally, calmly, and quietly, as at the "still point" of one's life.

The paradox of Japanese Zen is like a koan in its own right. It is the koan of Zen itself. Rinzai teaching and technique suggest a kind of Buddhism after the Fall. They offer a means of salvation and escape from the temptations of *maya* and the follies of *avidya* in the pit of *samsara*. By pursuing koan-zen under a qualified master, one may hope to be illuminated as to the true nature of one's predicament and be emancipated from that predicament by being rescued and returned to one's original nature and true home. Trapped as if by a pervasive condition of Original Sin, one nevertheless is moved by the dim remembrance of the primal Garden of one's being. "Man is forever seeking and grasping. Why? He grasps for the world because intuitively he longs to be rejoined with that from which he has been estranged through delusion."[17]

Soto on the other hand insists upon faith in a kind of prelapsarian state which is not a lost virtue or forgotten wholeness but an ever-present reality. That Original Goodness is not destroyed nor is it irretrievable, but it is the fundamental source of all good impulses and actions. There may be considerable dirt and debris scattered around the oasis of one's life, but the springs are still there, the water is pure, and if one will put down the bucket of zazen one will bring up the clear water of an inexhaustible underground stream. "Before Bodhidharma," comments Shunryu Suzuki, "people thought that after long preparation, sudden enlightenment would come. Thus Zen practice was a kind of training to gain enlightenment. . . . But this is not the traditional understanding of Zen—the understanding passed down from Buddha to our time is that when you start zazen, there is enlightenment even without any preparation. . . . Because you have [Buddha-nature], there is enlightenment in your practice."[18]

The language of Rinzai Zen is that of the surgeon. The patient is deathly ill and the most extreme measures are necessary to sever and remove the malignant growth. The disease is variously characterized in traditional Buddhist terms as ego, desire, attachment, ignorance, and dualistic thinking. Koan-meditation is the ideal surgical instrument for removing the cancer—a cancer, furthermore, that is usually understood as pervading one's whole being and is not likely to be treated by any other means. As Yasutani-roshi expressed it, "This 'I' is so powerfully embedded that it can't be uprooted by reasoning. In single-minded concentration on Mu you are not aware of 'I' standing against what is 'not-I'. If the absorption in Mu continues without interruption, the 'I-ness' dies out in the subconscious mind. Suddenly 'Plop!'—there is no more duality. To experience this directly is kensho."[19] Similarly, in speaking of the Mu koan, Yasutani's American disciple, Philip Kapleau, refers to it as "an exceptionally wieldy scapel for extirpating from the deepest unconscious the malignant growth of 'I' and 'not-I' which poisons the Mind's inherent purity and impairs its fundamental wholeness.''[20]

Once-born, Twice-born Psychologies

In sorting out these issues and differences, William James' classic distinction between once-born and twice-born religious experience would seem to offer some helpful insights. The distinction is an old one within the psychology of religion, older than James in point of theory, and probably as old as religion in point of fact. To be sure, it is a distinction which in James is applied to Western, largely Christian examples. It is also a distinction which seems an instance of the very dualism and discrimination which Zen speaks of transcending. Nevertheless, when one examines the reported religious experiences of representatives of the two Zen schools, from the pivotal figures of the two sects in Japan—Dogen (Soto) and Hakuin (Rinzai)—to present-day practitioners, they seem remarkably ''true to type.'' The respective teachings of both schools, their pedagogical methods, and their interpretations of meditation and enlightenment are quite consistent with the differences between a once-born and twice-born religious psychology. There has been some borrowing back and forth, and some internal ebb and flow of discipline and interpretation. But by and large the two schools in Japan and in the West have preserved their different emphases, and have sought to encourage corresponding types of experiences.

In his Gifford lectures of 1901-02 William James developed the typology of once-born and twice-born forms of religious experience and expression. It was a distinction which he had adopted from Francis Newman's work of a half-century earlier called *The Soul, its Sorrows and Aspirations.* ''God has two families of children on this earth,'' Newman had written, ''the once-born and the twice-born.'' The twice-born are those who have—in the context and categories of Christian belief—a profound sense of sin before a holy and omnipotent divinity, whereas the once-born ''see God, not as a strict Judge, not as a Glorious Potentate, but as the animating Spirit of a beautiful harmonious world.''[21]

William James, in his pioneering book *The Varieties of Religious Experience,* attempted to explore these two types of experience in less doctrinal and more psychological terms. Attention was focused on

16

the characteristics of the religious experiences themselves rather than on the various theological forms in which these experiences were expressed and by which they were interpreted. James also considerably elaborated upon Newman's distinction through designations such as "healthy-minded" and "sick-minded," the "harmonious self" and the "divided self." Those who were fundamentally good-natured, happy spirits, optimistic and accepting of the world, were the once-born. Not troubled by profound inner conflicts and experiencing no desperate need of salvation from their condition, the once-born tended to mature gradually and normally without any significant traumas, crises, or emotional extremes. Those, on the other hand, who were beset by deep-seated anxiety, melancholy, dread, doubt, and despair, or who were torn asunder by agonizing quandaries and antagonistic impulses, were the sick souls or divided selves—or worse, both—who hopefully might escape from this unhappy condition through some liberating rebirth and reconstitution of the psyche.

Though James expanded the purview of the discussion considerably, and cited a wide variety of cases in doing so, he limited himself to the Western, largely Christian, tradition. At one point in his lectures, James mentioned Buddhism in passing as a prime example of a "religion of salvation"—i.e., from a sick-souled, divided-self condition.[22] But in his descriptions and analyses of the healthy-minded, once-born type of experience, Buddhism did not come to mind as providing any examples; in his view it was already fully identified with the twice-born type. The issue remains, therefore, whether there are important instances in Buddhism of both types, and in particular whether James' typology may be helpful in elucidating the differences between Rinzai and Soto Zen.

Certainly Rinzai practitioners, from the time of Lin-chi (Rinzai, 8th century) to the present, have evidenced many of the characteristics which James associated with both the sick soul and the divided self: depression, anxiety, fear of death, numbness, insomnia, tension, conflict, fear of being alone, etc. During the intensive koan-meditation further symptoms often manifest themselves: doubt, hopelessness, despair, a sense of being alone and forsaken, fear of death (or fear of not being able to die). Finally, if the techniques are successful, a breakthrough occurs, likened to a volcanic eruption or an explosion, accompanied by shouting and laughing, and followed by a sense of victory over alien forces within, of liberation from an imprisonment, and of limitless joyful peace.

All these are common images in the testimonies of the (largely Christian) twice-born cases which James and others have cited. But they are also common images in the annals of Rinzai Zen and in the Zen records upon which the Rinzai school draws. The objective may be, and usually is, characterized by terms familiar to the twice-born: rebirth, regeneration, resurrection, revolution, revival. A modern Rinzai master, Shibayama Zenkei, teaches that the goal of Zen training is for the self "to die" and then to be "revived" as the self without form. Having been brought back from the depths into which one has been plunged by the koan, one can begin to live in the freedom of a "new man."[23]

Roshi Philip Kapleau is a contemporary American case in point. Kapleau's own situation on coming to Zen is quite revealing of the attraction and meaningfulness of Rinzai Zen to a certain type of person and circumstance. Kapleau was a 46-year-old businessman in New York City who was afflicted with ulcers and allergies, and who was unable to sleep without drugs. Life had become miserable and meaningless, and there were thoughts of suicide. In this situation Kapleau had read several books on Zen and had attended lectures given by the Rinzai scholar D.T. Suzuki. He had gained some intellectual understanding of the drift of Zen teaching, though it remained largely enigmatic, and there was no immediate sense of being personally affected by this knowledge. Yet it had begun to point him in what seemed to be a promising direction. He decided to go to Japan to study under a Zen master, hoping to experience what the Zen stories and teachings described. He resigned from his business, sold his car and furniture, and went to Japan in search of peace of mind and a purpose for being. After five years of practice under three masters, he eventually achieved a satori which dramatically changed his outlook and psychological state.

For most of his initial five years of Rinzai practice he had meditated on the Mu koan. One night both he and the roshi sensed that a breakthrough was near. As the roshi began speaking to him at the afternoon *dokusan,* saying "The universe is One. The moon of Truth. . ." Kapleau experienced a satori. "All at once the roshi, the room, every single thing disappeared in a dazzling stream of illumination and I felt myself bathed in a delicious, unspeakable delight. . . . For a fleeting eternity I was alone—I alone was. . . . Then the roshi swam into view. Our eyes met and flowed into each other, and we burst out laughing. . . . 'I have it! I know! There is nothing, absolutely nothing. I am everything and everything is nothing'."[24]

A few days later Kapleau describes the afterglow of his rebirth experience as follows: "Feel free as a fish swimming in an ocean of cool, clear water after being stuck in a tank of glue. . . . and so grateful (especially) for the privilege as a human being to know this Joy, like no other."[25]

Soto practitioners, in contrast, tend to evidence those characteristics which James associated with the healthy-minded, once-born type. The individual comes to Zen, not out of a sense of lostness and inner turmoil, but with a feeling of what is variously described as curiosity, inquisitiveness, fascination, exploration, intrigue, and a sense of mystery, expectancy, and adventure. The evidence points to people who are open to new worlds, are not easily threatened, are emotionally stable, who live life enthusiastically and enjoy life. They may experience brief periods of doubt, confusion, and uncertainty in their lives, but the source is largely external rather than internal, and they recover their poise and equilibrium quickly. They do not feel, nor are they encouraged to feel, a profound sense of alienation, inner contradiction, or anxiety. Zen practice and the Zen way have a feeling of naturalness about them. If there is a profound sensibility, it is that of being at home rather than being estranged or lost.

A contemporary Soto master, Charlotte Joko Beck, expresses her own realization of the meaning of Zen practice in a manner quite different from that of Philip Kapleau. "As we practice we see more and more clearly what we're really up to, how we cling to these walls we create. Doing zazen is not a matter of trying to get somewhere or become something; it is just to be here, fully experiencing each moment."[26]

The interpretive imagery itself is quite revealing in both contexts. In Rinzai cases the imagery is that of struggle and victory, conflict and resolution, bondage and liberation, lost and found, despair and elation, misery and joy. There is considerable mention of tension, crisis, trauma, alienation. Within is an adversary that must be squarely confronted, attacked, and defeated. The imagery, in fact, is often very militaristic. To quote Philip Kapleau again: "Your enemy is your discursive thinking, which leads you to differentiate yourself on one side of an imaginary boundary from what is not you on the other side of this non-existent line. . . . Your enemy is your own personal ego. When you have stopped thinking of yourself as a separated individuality and have realized the Oneness of all existence, you have dealt your ego a mortal blow."[27]

In Soto Zen the images are those of naturalness, at-homeness, harmony, tranquility, gentleness, purity, goodness, growth, nurturing. The emphasis is not on the dramatic and heroic but on the ordinary. One does not begin Zen practice with a quarrel or complaint, nor make of it a fight. The language is more musical than militaristic. In traditional Chinese terms, Rinzai is more *yang* in character (masculine, active, aggressive, bellicose), while Soto is more *yin* in character (feminine, passive, calm, quietistic).

In Soto one begins in the faith that one's practice—and one's very interest in Zen practice itself—is born from one's original nature, which is enlightened. Thus Master Obora, a 20th-century abbot of the Soto school, teaches: "When the life of faith manifests, it is the life of satori. He who enters into the state of faith is one who verily has entered the state of satori. He is awakened."[28] Shunryu Suzuki similarly teaches: "There is no need to understand what I say. You understand; you have full understanding within yourself. There is no problem."[29]

This is not to suggest that religious or philosophical questions are reducible to psychological states. But psychological elements are an important dimension of the total picture. One cannot abstract belief and practice from the psyche, any more than one can abstract mind from body. The conviction with which Rinzai and Soto masters and their followers have advocated their respective forms of Zen indicates a firm grounding in personal experience. One must also keep in mind the considerable emphasis in Buddhism, certainly foremost in Zen, upon the primacy of experience. Both Rinzai and Soto are in full agreement that the truths of Buddhism must above all be realized inwardly and lived outwardly, and that it is in these regions that such truths are tested, demonstrated, and brought to fulfillment.

CHAPTER II

Born-Again Buddhism: Hakuin

He is wise who deeply fears falling into hell. Only because the terrors of hell are so little known to them do men have no desire for the teachings of the Buddha.

Bassui[1]

In the past three hundred years, the most towering figure in Japanese Rinzai Zen has been Hakuin (1686-1769). Founded by Lin-chi (Rinzai) in China in the 9th century, Rinzai Zen began to develop in Japan in the 13th century, and justly celebrates a long line of notable masters in both lands. Hakuin is neither alone at the summit nor atypical. But because of the vividness and dramatic character of his religious experiences, the impress of his personality, his voluminous writings, and his literary gifts, Hakuin has been the dominant figure in Rinzai Zen from his time to the present. All contemporary Rinzai masters trace their dharma lineage to Hakuin, his koan-system, his methods of Zen practice, and his understanding of satori. Rinzai Zen in Japan is essentially Hakuin Zen.

The lives of the majority of Zen monks and masters are usually reported in brief and often enigmatic anecdotes. Such is the case with Kakua, reputedly one of the first Japanese to study Zen in China. Upon returning from China, he was requested to address the emperor concerning his experiences and learning; his elucidation is said to have consisted of producing a flute from the folds of his robe, blowing one short note, bowing, and walking out.[2] Fortunately, Hakuin has been more informative. In his writings he has provided detailed accounts of his religious experiences, and these accounts of his spiritual struggles are most revealing of the character of his Zen.

The first experience mentioned in Hakuin's *Orategama* already offers an autobiographical report familiar to the psychic odysseys of the twice-born. When Hakuin was seven or eight he was profoundly disquieted by a sermon delivered on the eight hot and eight cold hells described in a Tendai Buddhist text, the *Mo-ho chih-kuan.* "So vivid was the priest's description that it sent shivers down the spines of both monks and laymen, and made their hair stand on end in terror. Returning home, I took stock of the deeds of my short life and felt there was but little hope for me. I did not know which way to turn and was gooseflesh all over."[3] Secretly he began to chant passages from the *Lotus Sutra* "day and night," but to little avail. Even a hot bath and the crackling of the wood fire beneath so reminded him of the caldrons of the eight hot hells that he gave a shriek of terror heard throughout the neighborhood.

In Hakuin's impressionable mind his condition was so desperate that he became convinced that his only hope lay in monkhood. His parents refused to consider the proposition. Young Hakuin, however, continued to spend inordinate amounts of time at home and in the temple studying Confucian classics and reciting Buddhist sutras. His desire to become a monk only increased, and at fifteen he left home against his parents' wishes, throwing himself with great resolve into monastic religious practices. Yet the expected sense of peace and spiritual achievement did not come. Despite his most concerted efforts he seemed to be getting nowhere and became disheartened and "greatly depressed."

At the age of sixteen he reports that he was hounded by doubts concerning Buddhist scripture and practice. At nineteen he recollects deeper doubt and disillusionment as a result of an account he had read in a Zen text of Master Yen-t'ou, who had cried out when attacked and killed by bandits, thus seeming to give the lie to the promised peace and tranquillity of enlightenment. "What use was there in studying Zen? What a fraud Buddhism! How I regretted that I had cast myself into this band of strange and evil men. . . . So great was my distress that for three days I could not eat, and for a long time my faith in Buddhism was completely lost. Statues of the Buddha and the sacred scriptures looked like mud and dirt to me."[4]

In all this Hakuin manifested the characteristic turmoil to which William James applied the term *soul-sickness*. James described the symptoms as those of melancholy, fear, dread, depression, anxiety, guilt, anguish, despair.[5] All of these terms express the mental state reported by Hakuin. Hakuin also manifested the traits of what James termed the *divided self*. In this condition an individual experiences a profound inner conflict, perhaps feeling on the one hand wretchedly sinful and deserving of suffering, yet on the other hand possessed by an equally holy desire to be righteous. Religious efforts of the most diligent sort are confounded and sabotaged by desperate feelings of lostness, darkness, bondage, and doubt. There is often a heavy burden of guilt, yet over matters that to others may seem normal, minor, or even trifling.[6] Hakuin, for example, recalled being conscience-stricken over having committed the "heinous sins" of killing small birds and insects. This state is frequently accompanied by a sense of being tormented, or that one is going to be tormented. Nothing but a radical transformation in the depths of one's being would seem to offer any promise of salvation from such a depraved condition.

For Hakuin transformation and release were still some time in coming. It was not until he was twenty-two that he experienced his first awakening while listening to a Zen lecture, and later a more intense awakening while reading a Buddhist work. These experiences, however, are given no further elaboration and appear to have been quite preliminary stirrings, like tremors in advance of a major volcanic eruption. No revolutionary significance is attached to them. Hakuin comments only that he then began concentrating on the *Mu* koan "night and day. . . without a moment's rest," yet was deeply disappointed over his inability to maintain an unwavering concentration on *Mu*.

This state of affairs—ambiguous at best—persisted until, at the age of twenty-four, matters reached a breaking point which Hakuin later designated as the "Great Doubt" (*daigi*) and made one of the preconditions of enlightenment. "[I was] pursuing my strenuous studies. Night and day I did not sleep; I forgot both to eat and rest. Suddenly a great doubt manifested itself before me. It was as though I were frozen solid in the midst of an ice sheet extending tens of thousands of miles. . . . To all intents and purposes I was out of my mind and the *Mu* alone remained. Although I sat in the Lecture Hall and listened to the Master's lecture, it was as though I were hearing a discussion from a distance outside the hall. At times I felt as though I were floating through the air.''[7]

After several days in this condition, which he also later designated as the ''Great Death'' (*daishi*) and interpreted as the dying of ego and illusion, he recounted how he ''chanced to hear the sound of the temple bell and. . . was suddenly transformed. It was as if a sheet of ice had been smashed or a jade tower had fallen with a crash. Suddenly I returned to my senses. . . . All my former doubts vanished as though ice had melted away. In a loud voice I called: 'Wonderful! Wonderful!'.''[8]

To such an enlightenment experience Hakuin gave the designation the ''Great Joy'' (*daikangi*). The experience is later described as the ''joyous delight of that single victorious cry of 'Ka!' [in one who has] cut off the root-force of life—that cast of the mind of ignorance which has come down through countless past ages.''[9] In order to reach the heights of this ''Great Joy'' it was necessary to fall to the depths of ''Great Doubt.'' In fact, Hakuin argued, the intensity of joy and the degree of understanding were directly proportional to the intensity of doubt and the degree of dying to self that preceded it. ''If your doubt measures ten degrees so will your enlightenment.''[10] Or, ''at the bottom of great doubt lies great awakening. If you doubt fully you will awaken fully.''[11] In doubt, as it were, one sinks to the lowest pit of darkness and despair, and begins to realize the depths of one's fallen condition, like the prodigal son who finds himself eating husks with the swine. Note the remarkably similar comment made by William James: ''The rapturous sorts of happiness of which the twice-born make report has as an historic matter of fact been through a more radical pessimism than anything we have yet considered.''[12]

Hakuin also uses the twice-born imagery of death-and-rebirth. In the Buddhist context death-and-rebirth would more literally be understood as rebirth after death in another reincarnated form or in the heavenly paradise of Amida Buddha's Pure Land. For Hakuin, however, death-and-rebirth describes the satori event. One dies to self and to desire; former attachments are cut off; old illusions are destroyed; and one is reborn to new life, the life of Buddha. ''If you wish accordance with the true, pure non-ego, you must be prepared to let go your hold when hanging from a sheer precipice, to die and return again to life. . . . Then when suddenly you return to life, there is the great joy of one who knows for himself whether it is hot or cold. This is known as rebirth in the Pure Land. This is known as seeing into one's own nature.''[13] Only one who has experienced Great Doubt and Great Death can experience the Great Joy of new birth: *daigi, daishi, daikangi.*

Rebirth by Other-Power or Self-Power

This does not mean that Hakuin advocated a kind of "salvation by grace," a divine rescue of shipwrecked and drowning mortals. The other great Japanese example of a twice-born religious experience is, of course, that of Shinran (13th century). He was converted to Pure Land Buddhism after many years of searching and discontent, and represents the type of twice-born experience, so familiar within Christianity, in which spiritual rebirth is understood as being the result of an inbreaking saving power and insight, coming from *without.* Hakuin, on the other hand, understood his revolutionary experience as breaking forth from *within,* a sudden assertion of his innermost nature.

In Japanese these types are commonly expressed by the terms *tariki* (other-power) and *jiriki* (self-power). Hakuin is clearly as thorough-going an example of the *jiriki* understanding of his experience as Shinran is of the *tariki* understanding. Shinran saw his years of spiritual wandering as witness to the degeneracy of an age in which enlightenment, and even good and meritorious works which might lead to a favorable rebirth, were impossible. One's only hope was to have faith in the grace of Amida Buddha, who would carry all believers to his Western Paradise at death. Out of his infinite compassion he would rescue all who called upon his name from this evil land (*edo*) and take them to his Pure Land (*jodo*).

Hakuin's dramatic experience of liberation, joy and peace was interpreted in the opposite terms of a bursting forth of the Buddha-nature within (hence *jiriki,* self-power). He does not totally dismiss the images of the compassionate Buddha or rebirth in a Pure Land, but instead demythologizes them. For Hakuin the true meaning of rebirth in the Pure Land is to be born again out of the purity of "our own true and Original Self-Nature which presents itself in direct immediacy."[14] Or again, the Pure Land Buddhists "do not know that 'the West' signifies their own underived Mind-Root."[15]

Against those who argue that in this evil age of the declining dharma one can no longer make the necessary efforts to move toward enlightenment and must rely on the help of Amida Buddha, Hakuin uses the analogy of a prosperous farmer and his sons. The sons have inherited large land holdings from their father. But one son who is weak and lazy complains that it is no longer possible to imitate the labor and achievement of his ancestors: people no longer have the stamina, and the weeds and work seem overwhelming. There is, however, a Great Lord in another province who has abundant wealth and storehouses of grain, and who furthermore is exceptionally generous. If, the indolent son argues, we put on peasants' clothing and make a humble appearance, throwing ourselves on his mercy, out of his compassion and abundance he will provide for our wants and we need never toil again. So the other sons follow his counsel, abandon their father's fields, and appeal to the Great Lord. The result is that, though they could have enjoyed the wealth and satisfaction of their own labor, they become poor for the rest of their lives, their fields are choked with weeds, and they live idly on the welfare and achievement of another.[16]

Hakuin did not deny the value of the "Other Power" approach entirely, but saw it as a lesser way for lesser spirits: those who are weak, mediocre, lazy, impotent, cowardly—to cite some of the adjectives Hakuin freely and colorfully uses. Koan-zen was for heroic types, superior individuals possessed of great fortitude and zeal, determined to win through to enlightenment. In a letter on the relative merits of the koan and the chanting of the *nembutsu* (which, according to Shinran, would be efficacious if uttered but once with faith in the power of Amida Buddha to save), Hakuin comments in pointed fashion: "In Zen it is as though giants were pitted against one another, with victory going to the tallest. In Pure Land it is as though midgets were set to fight, with victory going to the smallest."[17]

As for chanting the *nembutsu*, Hakuin acknowledges some psychological value in the practice, but not the values accorded it in Pure Land teaching. It may function as a way of focussing the mind, moving away from ego-consciousness, and stepping out of the discriminating mind. Nonetheless, he quips, "calling the Buddha's

26

name is fine, but you could as well recite the grain grinding song instead."[18] There is also the danger that an emphasis upon faith in the salvation of Amida Buddha will turn one in the opposite direction from the Great Doubt which is an essential prelude to enlightenment. Hakuin talks frequently about the necessity of developing a "ball of doubt" (*gidan*), like a large knot tightly coiled in the pit of one's stomach. "The *Mu* Koan easily gives rise to the ball of doubt, while the recitation of the Buddha's name makes it very difficult to bring it to a head."[19]

Hakuin levels similar criticisms at the Nichiren sect with its advocacy of salvation through chanting the title of the Lotus Sutra, *(namu) Myoho renge kyo.* Like the *nembutsu,* if this were chanted and otherwise kept before the mind incessantly—in a manner similar to Hakuin's constant meditation upon a koan—this could become an acceptable practice, though lacking in the power generated by the paradoxical character of a koan. "Should a person wish to hold to this *Sutra,* he must throughout all the hours of the day and without the slightest doubt in his mind, carry on the real practice of true meditation on the total form of all things, thinking neither of good nor of evil."[20] The object of this chanting, however—as he has argued with respect to Amida Buddha—is not an Other-power external to the self. "What is being pointed out when we speak of the True Face of the Lotus? It is the Wondrous Law of the One Mind, with which you yourself are endowed from the start. It is nothing more than to see into your own mind [*kensho*]."[21]

The Battlefield of the Spirit

Ecstatic experiences continued to characterize Hakuin's Zen life for many years, leading to his belief that there was not just one enlightenment, but a succession of possible enlightenments—as in mining a rock quarry one does not break up all the stubborn strata with but one blast, or as in being awakened to the light one does not see everything, nor see with full clarity, at the first opening of one's eyes. In fact, his first satori was so ecstatic that his ego returned with greater force than ever. "My pride soared up like a majestic mountain, my arrogance surged forward like the tide. Smugly I thought to myself: 'In the past two or three hundred years no one could have accomplished such a marvelous breakthrough as this'."[22] Confident in his

27

attainment he then sought out Master Shoju to tell of his glorious enlightenment. Shoju was not impressed and, after testing him with a koan, twisted Hakuin's nose and said to him, "You poor hole-dwelling devil! Do you think somehow that you have sufficient understanding?"[23] After that incident, Hakuin reports, "almost every time he saw me, the Master called me a 'poor hole-dwelling devil'."[24]

Later sessions between Shoju and Hakuin contained the same verbal and physical abuse that often typifies the dramatic, sometimes violent approach of Rinzai Zen. When Hakuin once brought a Zen verse he had composed to demonstrate his understanding, Shoju denounced the words as "delusions and fancies," and when Hakuin responded in kind Shoju gave him "twenty or thirty blows with his fists." Shoju then pushed him off the veranda, where he lay "stretched out in the mud as though dead, scarcely breathing and almost unconscious." After regaining consciousness, he arose and bowed to the Master, but Shoju again yelled at him, "You poor hole-dwelling devil!"

Thoroughly rebuffed and bewildered, Hakuin intensified his koan meditation, "not pausing to sleep or eat." When he felt he had received another enlightenment, he went again to Shoju to have his insight tested and confirmed. Again Shoju rejected him and called him a "poor hole-dwelling devil." Then one day, when Hakuin had gone into town to beg for food, he was set upon by a madman who began beating him with a broom. Suddenly he understood the koan on which he had been working, and several other koans that had been troubling him. This time when he reported his understanding to the master, Shoju neither approved nor disapproved, but laughed in a pleasant manner, and stopped calling him a "poor hole-dwelling devil."

After this time Hakuin reports having a variety of enlightenment experiences. In one case he was reading from the anecdotal records and "was overcome with a great joy, as though a dark path had suddenly been illumined." In another case he gained an enlightenment from "the sound of snow falling." In yet another he was "overcome by a great surge of joy" while practicing walking meditation, when he "suddenly had an enlightenment greater than any I had had before." One of Hakuin's more colorful accounts deals with his enlightenment during a heavy rainstorm:

One day when I was passing through southern Ise
I ran into a downpour and the waters reached to
my knees. Suddenly I gained an even deeper
understanding of the verse on the Roundness of the
Lotus Leaf by Ta-hui. I was unable to contain my
joy. I lost all awareness of my body, fell headlong
into the waters, and forgot completely to get up
again. My bundles and clothing were soaked
through. Fortunately a passerby, seeing my
predicament, helped me to get up. I roared with
laughter and everyone there thought I was mad. [25]

All was not, however, a succession of spiritual summits and
unspeakable ecstasies. After his first satori—despite the claim that
"all my old doubts melted away down to their very roots," that "the
age-old karma-root of birth-and-death was erased utterly," and that
he had spent "some months lost in dancing joy"—he eventually came
down from the mountain peak to another period of doubt and fear.
"I looked at my life [and saw that] the spheres of activity and stillness
were not at all in harmony; I found I was not free to either take up
a thing or leave it." [26] Again he determined to engage fervently and
relentlessly in religious practice, with the result that he eventually
became ill and was in a worse physical and mental state than before.

Teeth clenched and eyes aglaze, I sought to free
myself from food and sleep. Before a month had
passed the heart-fire mounted to my head, my lungs
were burning but my legs felt as if freezing in ice
and snow. In my ears was a rushing sound as of
a stream in a valley. My courage failed and I was
in an attitude of constant fear. I felt spiritually
exhausted, night and day seeing dreams, my arm-
pits always wet with sweat and my eyes full of
tears. I cast about in every direction, consulting
famous teachers and doctors, but all their devices
availed nothing at all. [27]

Only aged twenty-nine, Hakuin suffered what may have been a
nervous breakdown, a so-called "Zen sickness" not uncommon in
the context of a rigorous and sometimes traumatic Rinzai discipline.
In Hakuin's case the illness is hardly surprising, given both his
psychological history and the extremes of practice and emotion to

which he was given. Certainly there seems to have been an abrupt mood swing in the reversion from the very manic state after his first satori back to the depressive state which had preceded it.

Interestingly, at this point in his life he did not seek or find a cure for his mental condition in Zen but rather in Taoism. Desperate for help, Hakuin left Zen practice for a time and travelled to the cave of a Taoist hermit, Hakuyu, who lived in the mountains north of Kyoto. Reputed to be two hundred years old, the hermit was noted for his knowledge of Taoist medicine and therapy. The old hermit prescribed various methods for curing his condition, including frequent recitation of a certain Taoist formula and a kind of therapeutic introspection known as *naikan*. After three years of treatment Hakuin realized a cure and, now thirty-two, he returned to occupy his home temple, Shoin-ji, in his native town of Hara.

In the Rinzai context again, Hakuin resumed his koan-meditation and sought thereby further satoris. A satori in Rinzai is not seen as a once-for-all, total, finished experience. It is a moment in a process of ever deepening and widening one's understanding. The Buddhist Dharma may be likened to a great work of art that can never be completely seen and appreciated on first sight, but seems inexhaustible, so that each time one returns to it one sees something more, something new. Or, to use a very different simile which expresses the condition of the seeker after the Dharma, the Rinzai practitioner may be likened to a deathly-sick individual, suffering from many diseases, whose recovery will not only take an extended period of time but will require a number of medicines, therapies, and healings.

Hakuin quotes his own master, Shoju, who said that it was thirty-five years after his first awakening that he had attained the state where he could meditate in a pure manner. Hakuin, in his *Yasenkanna,* also cites the case of the Chinese master, Ta-hui, who had eighteen great satoris along with innumerable lesser ones. This was further attested, for Hakuin, by his own experience of many awakenings. After an initial awakening, therefore, it was most important to continue unrelenting koan-practice to the end of ever profounder insight. Hakuin and his followers organized and systematized this process by advocating a series of koans which one must "pass" and "move on" to another. After the master acknowledged one's initial awakening, following a period of meditation on a starter koan such as "Mu" or the "Sound of One Hand Clapping," one was assigned another koan, etc. In a very formal way, the Rinzai approach is not unlike a twice-born Christianity in which, after the initial experience of conversion and "justification," one is to continue the process in a deepening of one's understanding and a sanctification of one's life through prayer, bible study, devotion, and periodic revival.

The satori experiences that suddenly came upon Hakuin produced insights related not only to koans but to the Buddhist scriptures. One of the sutras that had troubled him in his earlier years had been the *Lotus Sutra*. Some time after the previously mentioned experiences, Hakuin again read the *Lotus*. "Suddenly I penetrated to the perfect, true, ultimate meaning of the Lotus. The doubts which I had held initially were destroyed and I became aware that the understanding I had obtained up to then was greatly in error. Unconsciously I uttered a great cry and burst into tears."[28] It was with this new understanding of the *Lotus Sutra* that he undertook to criticize Nichiren-sho-shu for its "vain chanting" of the title of the sutra.

It is quite apparent, in fact, that the vividness of Hakuin's Zen experiences, their sudden and decisive character, and their considerable contrast with previous states of doubt, fear, anxiety, and depression, provided him with a kind of irrefutable self-assurance. The boldness of his writings, the tenacity of his spirit, the rigors of his discipline, and the absolute conviction of his advocacy, bear witness to overwhelming experiences whose insights were, to him, self-evident and self-authenticating penetrations of "the perfect, true, ultimate meaning" of things. And the vividness of such experiences very easily became persuasive and inspirational for those who came in contact with such a charismatic master.

The Twice-Born Biography

One of the characteristics of autobiographies of the twice-born is that they make good stories—which is also the reason they tend to predominate in religious literatures. Unlike the more commonplace autobiographies of the once-born—if these are reported at all—they make for "good press." There are dramatic conflicts, titanic confrontations, exuberant passions, emotional extremes, stark contrasts, heroic struggles. There are powerful temptations to be overcome, tortuous ordeals to be passed through, awesome heights to climb, and terrible abysses to fall into. Extraordinary sensations, supranormal visions, ecstatic transports, dreams and fantasies are the stuff that twice-born tales are made of. Whether in mythological, legendary, or biographical form, such odysseys almost completely dominate religious traditions, whose duty it is to retell and re-enact them so that we may pattern our own existences after them. Modern psychological and existential literatures have similarly tended to focus on abnormal psychic odysseys, ignoring the more normal and less interesting cases in favor of the more extreme and presumably more "authentic" examples.

Hakuin's biography is not atypical of the biographies of noted Rinzai masters in both China and Japan, except that his account of it is more detailed and exuberant. The life of one of the early notables of Japanese Rinzai, Bassui Tokusho (1327-1387), for example, reads in a similar fashion. According to his disciple-biographer, Myodo, Bassui's mother had a vision during her pregnancy that her child would be possessed of an evil spirit and would turn against and kill his parents. At birth his mother abandoned him in a field, from which a servant rescued him and secretly raised him. The orphaned Bassui displayed at an early age a sensitive and questioning mind with respect to religious matters. Particularly troubling to him were the issues of the existence of a soul and the torments of hell. From the age of seven he was increasingly obsessed with such issues and beset by anxieties and fears. At the age of ten he would be wakened suddenly by the sensation of brilliant flashes of light in his room, followed by the feeling of being shrouded in thick darkness. For hours he would sit, as if in a daze, transfixed by the question—which he later described as a koan—"What is it within me which this very moment is seeing and hearing?" After years of searching he eventually experienced under the guidance of a Zen master a profound transformation that initially left him weeping for hours as if all his former troublings were being poured out in tears. He was, says his biographer, like "a barrel whose bottom had been smashed open."

One sees similar elements in the various stories which inspired Hakuin in his quest, or which he uses as exemplary models for his monks to emulate. During his own early searchings, Hakuin had been deeply stirred by the story of the Ch'an master Sekiso Soen (Shih-shuang Ch'u-yuan) who meditated for long hours, keeping a sharp awl beside him to stab his flesh should he start to doze. To his monks Hakuin held up the image of Gudo, who "went one very hot day to a grove of bamboo and sat in meditation without a stitch of clothing covering his body. At night great swarms of mosquitoes surrounded him and covered his skin with bites. Fighting. . . against the hideous itching, he gritted his teeth, clenched his fists, and simply sat as though mad. Several times he almost lost consciousness, but then unexpectedly he experienced a great enlightenment."[29]

Hakuin also cites the case of the Buddha who, in his six-year quest for true understanding, reduced himself to skin and bones, nearly starving to death; or the second Ch'an patriarch Hui-k'o, who reputedly cut off his forearm in demonstration of his utter determination to find peace of mind. Hakuin's own master, Shoju, used to tell the story of how he went to meditate for seven nights in the graveyards upon learning that a wolf pack was marauding in the vicinity. According to him, the prowling about of the wolves and their sniffing at his ears and throat tested his ability to sustain unwavering concentration.

This seemingly fanatical relentlessness is clearly in the tradition of Mumon, one of the early Chinese advocates of koan-practice and author of the widely-used collection of koans, the *Mumonkan*. Mumon is said to have worked on the Mu koan for six years before his first satori. In his commentary on the Mu koan, he says that to break through the barrier of Mu to the experience of enlightenment beyond its gate, "you must concentrate day and night, questioning yourself through every one of your 360 bones and 84,000 pores." He also says that you must be like one who has "swallowed a red-hot iron ball that you cannot disgorge despite your every effort."[30]

With this perspective in view, it is to be expected that Hakuin would advocate a strict, uncompromising discipline. He was intolerant of anything less than total, unflinching effort and determination. He frequently complained of the lack of seriousness and sincerity among so many monks of his day. Nothing was more despicable to him than to turn Buddhism into "a sweet and simple thing." The "Great Matter" of realizing the Buddha Dharma required nothing less than heroic struggle. His advice in a letter to a sick monk in the *Orategama* is characteristic of the unrelenting zeal which he insisted upon, in spite of the most adverse conditions. Even sickness should be used as an impetus for furthering one's practice rather than as an excuse for relaxing it for a moment. "Persistent practice at the times one is suffering from illness is essential. . . . No idleness can be tolerated."

Hakuin's letter quotes at great length the advice given by "an old monk" (probably his master, Shoju) to a sick monk (possibly Hakuin himself). Using illustrations from his own life and from that of others, the old monk argues that "for effective meditation nothing is better than practice when one is ill." Sickness is one of the many ordeals through which one may have to pass, and through which one's resolve is tested. "Even if surrounded by snakes and water spirits, a man, once he has determined to do something, must resolve not to leave unfinished what he has started. No matter how cold or hungry he may be, he must bear it; no matter how much wind and rain may come, he must withstand it. Even if he must enter into the heart of fire or plunge to the bottom of icy waters, he must open the eye that the Buddhas and Patriarchs have opened."[31]

As is already evident, the imagery which Hakuin uses or cites in his teaching is heroic, often violent, and one might say militaristic in character. Life is a battleground of contending forces, requiring spiritual warriors and the techniques of warfare. The enemies of ego, desire, attachment, and ignorance may throw every conceivable roadblock and pitfall in one's way. One may be assaulted from every side by the forces of Mara. Therefore "at all times in your study of Zen," he counsels, "*fight against* delusions and worldly thoughts, *battle* the *black demon* of sleep, *attack* concepts of active and passive, order and disorder, right and wrong, hate and love, and *join battle* with all things of the mundane world. Then in *pushing forward* with true meditation and *struggling fiercely,* there unexpectedly will come true enlightenment"[32] [italics mine]. Speaking of the role of the master in producing a highly enlightened and worthy successor, Hakuin uses imagery that would make even the toughest drill sergeant quake: "He lets reverberate in his mouth the talons and teeth of the Cave of Dharma, smashes the brains of monks everywhere, pulls out the nails and knocks out the wedges."[33]

Zen anecdotes are notorious for their shocking and abusive language, even in dealing with such sacred matters as the Buddha, scripture, and patriarchs. And in cultures like the Chinese and Japanese which have placed so great an emphasis upon courtesy, respect, and decorum, such Zen language must appear as doubly rough and improper. "What a mess are the Three Vehicles (the *Triyana*), the teachings of the twelve divisions of the Canon, and Bodhidharma's coming from the West!" "The Buddha is a bull-headed jail-keeper, and the Patriarchs are horse-faced old maids." "The Buddha is a shit-stick." "Kill the Buddha."

Hakuin, similarly, was a master of shocking and abusive language. The titles of some of his works are provocative, to say the least. His commentary on the *Hannya Shingyo* (the Heart Sutra) was entitled *Dokugo* ("poisonous words of") *Hannya Shingyo*. To anyone who represented a position which he saw as weakening or distorting Buddhism, or who seemed guilty of half-heartedness in the Buddhist way, Hakuin was a veritable thesaurus of insult and invective. A barrage of verbal assaults fill his writings as he attacks viewpoints and practices which he sees as threatening Buddhism from within or without. Opponents are called idiots, fools, blind, stupid, ignorant, miserable, moronic, worm-like, deluded, trifling, heretics. At the least Hakuin may be said to have had a bold and exuberant style!

Such a vigorous vocabulary corresponds to the intense nature of his own spiritual struggles and experiences, and the intensity with which he lived. The front lines of the battle with the kingdom of Mara is no place for cowards and weaklings, and in the thick of the fray one does not use soft words and idle pleasantries. In a lengthy letter to the Governor of Settsu Province, Hakuin argues that "the advantage in accomplishing true meditation lies distinctly in the favor of the warrior class. A warrior must from the beginning to the end be physically strong. . . . The valiant, undaunted expression on his face reflects his practice of the peerless, true, uninterrupted meditational sitting."[34] Clearly for him Zen was fundamentally a matter of spiritual warfare; the monk was to be seen as a spiritual warrior; and the warrior virtues were essential in winning the victory. It would be too much to say flatly that this is Samurai Zen; but in spirit, in values, in imagery—and by analogy—it is *bushido*, the warrior's way.

It is no surprise, then, to find that the pedagogical techniques used by Hakuin are similarly dramatic, conflict-centered, and crisis-oriented. On the basis of his own twice-born experiences and those commonly reported in the Zen anecdotal tradition, Hakuin's mission is to precipitate similar experiences in his monks and lay followers. Some of the techniques used are evident in the story of Shoju's treatment of the young monk Hakuin. By verbal abuse, physical abuse, rejection and frustration, the psyche of the novice is brought to a breaking point beyond which, hopefully, will come light and liberation.

Zen anecdotes, particularly those stressed in Rinzai, frequently refer to "roughhouse" treatment: shouting, slapping, striking, kicking, beating. Rinzai himself was noted for his "lion's roar" with which he deafened his monks, sometimes for three days! And in the formal use of the kyosaku stick in striking monks during periods of meditation, Rinzai Zen makes a more vigorous and prolonged use of the instrument than does Soto Zen. The object in all such techniques is that of doing a kind of violence to the self and to ordinary ways of thinking and perceiving. Ego, desire, attachment and illusion are, as it were, beaten out of the practitioner.

The most important technique, however, is the koan. This is the principal weapon used in the battlefield of the spirit. So important does the koan become that meditation is largely understood as meditation on a koan (*kanna-zen*). In this manner one totally frustrates and thwarts the enemy: illusory ways of thinking and being. The defenses of the ego are collapsed; desire is assaulted; and a crisis in consciousness is brought about. The value of the koan is that by means of an enigmatic statement, contradictory assertion, nonsensical remark, or unintelligible action, a seemingly irreconcilable conflict situation is set up—not unlike the dramatic and apparently unresolvable conflicts which are the basic tragic structure of many Japanese Noh dramas. One is to meditate on a koan until one's intellection is wearied, one's rationality is thoroughly confounded, and one's spirit is broken. At "wit's end" one may then, for Hakuin, be able to experience that Great Doubt and Great Death which lead to Great Joy and the victorious cry of "Ka!"

In the *Yabukoji* Hakuin speaks in the following way about the koan "What is the Sound of One Hand Clapping?" which he had devised for his monks: "In the place where reason is exhausted and words are ended, you will suddenly pluck out the karmic root of birth and death and break down the cave of ignorance. . . . At this time the basis of mind, consciousness and emotion is suddenly shattered; the realm of illusion with its endless sinking into the cycle of birth and rebirth is overturned."[35]

Hakuin's understanding of Zen practice is not only the result of his positive experiences with koan-meditation, but also his negative experiences with the practice of "zazen alone" favored by the Soto school. In the early years of his monastic practice, he had tried the more quietistic approach of sitting calmly and emptying his mind in accord with Buddhist teachings on emptiness (*sunyata*), non-action (*mui*), and no-thought (*mushin*). He had believed that "absolute tranquillity of the source of the mind was the Buddha Way." But the more he tried to achieve this state of mind, the less tranquil his mind became. The more he sought to realize the state of emptiness, the more his thoughts and emotions were filled from all directions.

> Trivial and mundane matters pressed against my chest and a fire mounted in my heart. I was unable to enter wholeheartedly into the active practice of Zen. My manner became irascible and fears assailed me. Both my mind and my body felt continually weak, sweat poured endlessly from my armpits, and my eyes constantly filled with tears. My mind was in a continual state of depression and I made not the slightest advance toward gaining the benefits that result from the study of Buddhism.[36]

Because of Hakuin's failure in the zazen-only approach and his subsequent successes with the koan method, he became a passionate advocate of the koan and an arch-critic of what he called "dead sitting" (*shiza*) and the "silent-illumination (*mokusho*) heretics" that practiced it. Of his former, failed approach he says: "[They] foolishly take the dead teachings of no-thought and no-mind, where the mind is like dead ashes with wisdom obliterated, and make these into the essential doctrines of Zen. They practice silent, dead sitting as though they were incense burners in some old mausoleum."[37] As Hakuin saw it, a part of the problem was that without a koan to focus upon the sitting accomplishes very little, because one tends either to go to sleep or to let the mind wander. "They sit in meditation for one minute and fall asleep for a hundred, and during the little bit of meditation that they manage to accomplish, their minds are beset by countless delusions. As soon as they set their eyes, grit their teeth, clench their fists, adjust their posture, and start to sit, ten thousand evil circumstances begin to race about in their minds."[38]

Hakuin also objected to the passivity of the zazen-only approach. For him, Zen practice was *practice;* it was active, aggressive, dynamic. Focussing on the koan forced one to attack the problem, come to grips with it, wrestle it to the ground. Taking hold of a koan was like taking hold of the horns of a raging bull; one could hardly sit out the encounter as if one were contemplating a rose garden. One must be totally preoccupied with the bull, without a moment's rest, until the bull is subdued or killed—and until the next bull is brought into the ring. Just sitting, however, is like trying to become a great bull-fighter by sitting in the middle of the ring without a bull, smelling flowers. The analogy is not Hakuin's, but approximates his concern with "those fools who starve to death on mountains, thinking that dead sitting and silent illumination suffice, and that Zen consists of the source of the mind being in tranquillity."[39] They are like "dead silkworms in their cocoons."

So much did Hakuin emphasize the active approach that he insisted that the center of Zen was not sitting in meditation upon a koan, but meditation on the koan itself, whether one was sitting, standing, walking, or working. If anything, he argued, meditation on the koan in the midst of daily activity was superior to sitting meditation for "penetrating to the depths of one's own self-nature, and for attaining a vitality valid on all occasions."[40] The energy of the koan could combine with the energy of one's daily tasks (*samu*) to provide a wholly active and dynamic movement toward deeper insight.

Nothing could have fit Hakuin's personality or personal experience better. None of the contexts, in fact, in which Hakuin reports having had enlightenment experiences mention zazen. Rather, he was busy with Zen studies, reading anecdotal records, listening to a lecture, doing walking meditation, wading through deep water in a rainstorm, examining the *Lotus Sutra*, observing a snowfall.

> What is true meditation? It is to make everything: coughing, swallowing, waving the arms, motion, stillness, words, action, the evil and the good, prosperity and shame, gain and loss, right and wrong, into one single koan.[41]

CHAPTER III

Once-Born Zen: Dogen

The essential functioning of Buddhas and Patriarchs
Is manifest without deliberation
And is accomplished without hindrance. . . .

The realization that is neither absolute nor relative
Penetrates without conscious intent.
Clear water soaks into the earth;
The fish swims like a fish.

Dogen[1]

In Japanese Zen the great advocate of "zazen-only" was Dogen, the founder of the Soto school in Japan. Dogen (1200-1253) had, in fact, begun his practice under the first Japanese teachers of Rinzai Zen, Eisai and his disciple Myozen. He had further travelled to China to study under several Lin-chi (Rinzai) masters. But it was only when he encountered a Chinese master of the Ts'ao-tung (Soto) School, Ju-ching, that he found a method and teaching which he felt to be fully authentic. He came to abandon koan usage as such in favor of "single-minded intense sitting" (*shikantaza*).

Though Dogen had done koan-meditation for many years, and very diligently so, he came to believe that meditation on koans could be a form of the "gradualist heresy," despite its great emphasis upon sudden enlightenment. If koan-zen was done in the expectation that one might thereby arrive at a marvelous enlightenment and, through working on further koans, progressively attain Buddhahood, it suggested a dualistic technique by means of which future spiritual goals might be attained. It would be like fruit ripening to the point where it would abruptly detach itself and fall from the tree of illusion and ignorance in a sudden satori.

Dogen came to teach instead that one should "just sit," for what one is attempting to realize one already *is* at the center of one's being. One already *is* a Buddha, *is* enlightened, *is* fundamentally at peace. One should therefore "just sit" within one's Buddha-nature and allow it to flow out into all of one's being and life. So, whereas Hakuin talks about "dead sitting" (*shiza*), Dogen talks about "just sitting," "total sitting," "nothing other than sitting" (*shikantaza*). Such sitting is by no means futile or dead, for it is a sitting within the fullness of the life of the Buddha. Even if one sits for but a short time in the shallows of the ocean of enlightenment, one nevertheless is sitting within the infinite expanse of that ocean.

In the *Zuimonki* Dogen counsels his monks: "Students must concentrate on zazen alone and not bother about other things. The Way of the Buddhas and Patriarchs is zazen only. Follow nothing else." With respect to koan-usage, on the other hand, he remarks: "Although a slight understanding seems to emerge from examining the koan, it causes the Way of the Buddhas and Patriarchs to become even more distant. If you devote your time to doing zazen without wanting to know anything and without seeking enlightenment, this is itself the Patriarchal Way." On the relative value of koan-zen and zazen, Dogen concludes: "Although the old Masters urged both the reading of the scriptures and the practice of zazen, they clearly emphasized zazen. Some gained enlightenment through the koan, but the merit that brought enlightenment came from zazen. Truly the merit is in the zazen."[2]

Sitting as the Buddha sat, one activates one's Buddha-nature. This is not "gradual enlightenment" as opposed to "sudden enlightenment," for enlightenment is the logical and ontological basis of all practice of the Way. To be able to sit in the faith that one is sitting in the Way of the Buddha and within one's own Buddha-nature implies that to some extent one is enlightened, otherwise one would simply consider it a theoretical possibility or doubt it entirely.

Faith itself is born of enlightenment, proceeds from enlightenment, and is one of the marks of enlightenment. Implicitly faith is already understanding and is drawn by this awareness of itself to become altogether conscious and explicit. It is not as though—as understood in koan-zen—one sits in the faith and hope that someday the practice of meditation will eventually and at long last lead to a satori and kensho. For Dogen this very desire and intention to sit, and this act of sitting, is already enlightenment and the Way of the Buddha and Patriarchs. It is not merely a path *to* enlightenment but the path *of* enlightenment. It is the enlightened way of being and doing. Zazen itself is sitting on the Diamond throne of the Buddha under the Bodhi tree.

This, in summary, is Dogen's "once-born" philosophy and practice. A close examination of his life shows the same close correlation between his experience and teaching as between Hakuin's twice-born experience and subsequent teaching.

Early Life

Dogen's youth already manifests the personality traits and perspective on life which William James associated with the once-born. Dogen's father, Koga Michicika, was an 8th-generation descendant of the Emperor Murakami (reigned 946-57). His father belonged to a branch of the distinguished Minamoto family and was Lord Keeper of the Privy Seal. His mother was of the Fujiwara clan, the court family which had been so prominent in the aristocracy of Japan for several centuries. Dogen was raised, therefore, in the highly refined atmosphere of the imperial court, imbued with its social graces, encouraged to become well-versed in Chinese and Japanese classics, and trained in the literary and poetic skills that were among the essentials of aristocratic intercourse.

Dogen was a precocious child, able to read Chinese poetry by the age of four and showing great promise for a distinguished career in court. Though he later set aside this direction and the luxury and aestheticism of courtly life, he had enjoyed exceptional privileges and opportunities. The refinements of courtly culture, the love of language, the classical training, and the literary graces remained with him and gave a breadth of perspective and richness of nuance to his works.

Dogen's childhood was not, however, altogether tranquil and bright. If anything, the misfortunes of his early life, the prevailing fatalistic mood of the age, and the pessimistic religious influences upon him could easily have led to a twice-born scenario. His father died when Dogen was two; his mother when he was seven. The impermanence of life (*mujo*) was a central theme in the literature of

41

the Heian period, influenced partly by Buddhist teachings regarding change and ephemerality and partly by aristocratic reflections on the brevity and vicissitudes of life. The death of Dogen's father had only impressed him in retrospect, but the death of his mother was striking confirmation of the transciency of life which court literature and Buddhist doctrine combined to stress.

Dogen's mother had made a dying request that he become a monk and search out the eternal truths of Buddhism rather than pursue the temporal matters of the court. Though his mother's brother wished to adopt him and train him for a career in the imperial house, Dogen chose instead at the age of twelve to follow his mother's last wish and become a monk. It was, in fact, not unusual in this period for members of the aristocracy who had suffered misfortune to renounce the world and enter a monastery. Dogen gave the death of his mother and her departing wish as his reasons for taking monastic vows. Dogen's personal journal (the *Hokyo-ki*) contains the comment that "at his mother's death, observing the smoke of the incense, he intimately realized the impermanence of the world of sentient beings, and profoundly developed the great aspiration to seek the Dharma."[3] At the age of thirteen, accordingly, he was initiated at the large center of Tendai Buddhism on Mt. Hiei, east of Kyoto.

The death of his mother did not, however, lead to some deep spiritual crisis or a pessimistic view of the world. Nor did the heightened sense of the transciency of life lead to melancholy. Human existence, no matter how brief, was seen as a great opportunity. As the above quotation phrases it, these circumstances "profoundly developed the great aspiration to seek the Dharma." Much later he was to write in the *Shukke kudoku* (Merit of Becoming a Monk) portion of the *Shobogenzo:* "Life is as ephemeral as a dewdrop, and so, having been fortunate enough to be born as a human being, we should not waste our lives."[4]

Dogen's monastic career was characterized by considerable energy and diligence in the learning and pursuit of the Buddhist Way. "I was blessed with a good karma," gratefully writes Dogen as a young man in his journal. One has the distinct impression of singleness of purpose, constancy of zeal and direction, eagerness and enthusiasm of spirit, a positive approach to issues, and a naturalness in his religious practice. Instead of being influenced by the fatalism and

42

melancholy that marked the spirit of the age in both its secular and religious literature, he moved forward in gratitude for the privilege of human birth and the present moment that was available to him. Life was perceived as a gift and a blessing, not a prisonhouse or battle-ground or cruel fate. Later he was to write: "Now that we have had the good fortune not only to be born in this world but also to come into contact with the Buddha Sakyamuni, how can we be anything but overjoyed!. . . . How fortunate to have been born in the present day, when we are able to make this encounter!"[5]

Dogen also resisted the temptation to give credence to the popular Pure Land teaching that all now lived in the degenerate third age of the Dharma (*mappo*), in which it was supposedly no longer possible to be enlightened or even to live a meritorious life in the hope of rebirth in a more favorable time and place—thus one's only hope was rebirth in Amida Buddha's Western Paradise through faith in his infinite merit and compassion. Dogen lived in the same century (the 13th) as the most radical exponent of Pure Land teaching, Shinran, founder of the *Jodo-shin-shu* (True Pure Land School). In fact, they had both been monks at one time in the same Tendai monastery on Mt. Hiei. Shinran's own difficulties, over many years of monastic training, in making spiritual progress and realizing the peace of mind promised in Buddhism, coupled with the general spirit and character of the age, led him to read his circumstances and those of the world surrounding him as proof that the dark age of Degenerate Dharma had come, or was shortly coming. In the first age of Right Dharma (*shobo*)—on this schema the first 500 years after the Buddha's enlightenment—it had been possible to follow the Buddha's teachings and achieve enlightenment. In the second age of Declining Dharma (*seppo*)—the next 1500 years—it was no longer possible to be enlightened, but one could pursue various meritorious acts in the hope that one might obtain thereby a more favorable rebirth in the presence of the Buddha of the West. But as the age continued to decline, it was harder and harder to do meritorious works that might assure one's entry, until in the third age of Degenerate Dharma—the next 3000 years—only one's faith in the infinite merit and compassion of the Buddha of the West could bring entry into his Pure Land. Thus did Shinran's very pessimistic view of himself and his age lead to a surprisingly optimistic result: since there was nothing one *could* do to achieve this salvation.

there was nothing one *needed* to do, except cast oneself on the mercy and grace of Amida Buddha.

Dogen acknowledged that there were various difficulties in being born so far away, both temporally and spatially, from the historical Buddha. One might lament the fact that one had not been born in the 6th century B.C. in northeastern India, that one had not been able to walk and talk with the Buddha, to receive direct guidance, or to feel the compelling power of his presence. One might lament the separation that comes about from so many intervening ages, cultures, languages, interpreters, and sects. Understandably one might despair of being able to comprehend the Buddha's Dharma correctly or practice it properly or pursue it diligently. All this might be persuasive except that, for Dogen, even though one might be 2000 years removed from the historical Buddha and his teachings, in a more fundamental sense one was *equidistant* from the Buddha and his Dharma, for one's true nature *is* Buddha and Dharma. It is toward this inner reality that the teachings of all the Buddhas point. When one sits in zazen, one sits in the presence of Buddha and realizes the Dharma.

One is reminded here in particular of William James' description of the positive religious outlook of the once-born, even in the face of harsh realities and pessimistic readings of life. They persist in "flinging themselves upon their sense of the goodness of life, in spite of the hardships of their own condition, and in spite of the sinister theologies into which they may be born. From the outset their religion is one of union with the divine."[6] The position at which Dogen eventually arrived offers the most direct challenge to excuses based on the misfortunes of life, the doubtfulness of significant achievement in such a brief life-span, the seemingly arduous path to enlightenment, or the degeneracy of the age. Buddhahood, enlightenment, and the purity and peace of nirvana are all aspects of one's original, innermost nature. "Those who have faith in the Way should know for certain that they are unfailingly in the Way from the beginning—thus free from confusions, delusions, being upside down, increase and decrease, and errors."[7]

In twice-born Zen the emphasis is upon *maya*, *avidya*, and *samsara*—the state of illusion and delusion, of egoism and desire, of false thinking and acting, from which the aspirant seeks deliverance. In once-born Zen the emphasis is upon one's original nature, which

44

is one's true and ever-present self, intrinsically pure and harmonious. In twice-born Zen truth and reality are to be discovered in what that great twice-born era of the 1960s came to call an "altered state of consciousness." In once-born Zen a non-dualistic consciousness is one's basic state of awareness-being out of which one is invited to live as a present capacity.

For Dogen there may be a moment when one first becomes self-consciously aware of what one already is and knows, returns to that, dedicates onself to that. One's "Dharma eye is opened." But if so, one should not make too much fuss over the experience of discovering what one already knows, or dwell on the excitement of finding what one already possesses. Such a moment is also not necessarily the result of a crisis of consciousness in which one's whole outlook and existence have been revolutionized. It is more like the moment in which a sleeping Buddha awakens and opens his eyes. A Buddha does not awaken from non-Buddhahood into Buddhahood, but out of his Buddhahood. And, as Master Bankei put it, whether asleep or awake a Buddha is still a Buddha.

Original and Acquired Enlightenment

Early in Dogen's monastic studies one question had troubled him, and it is the key to his Zen understanding. If, as Mahayana Buddhism teaches, we are all endowed with the Dharma from birth, and are therefore already in the truth, why is it necessary for all—even those exalted beings called Buddhas—to seek enlightenment and pursue arduous spiritual disciplines? In Mahayana Buddhism a distinction had been developed between original enlightenment (*hongaku*) and acquired enlightenment (*shikaku*). The Tendai sect in which Dogen had begun his monastic practice had given special emphasis to original enlightenment. And by Dogen's time Tendai teaching had carried the doctrine to the radical conclusion that enlightenment was an eternal reality, not a temporal occurrence. A parallel doctrine, "this body itself is Buddha" (*sokushin-jobutsu*), was likewise radicalized—in Japanese Tendai especially—leading to the conclusion that this life and the forms of this world were themselves Buddha, and therefore holy and liberated.

If such teachings were correct, what was the place or purpose of religious practice? Why any special exertion at all, let alone a long road of exertion in the hope of being enlightened and achieving nirvana? In fact, by the late Heian period such doctrines were commonly used by worldly Tendai monks to rationalize selfish interests and secular ambitions. Receiving no satisfactory answer to his conundrum from his own teacher, Dogen went on the abbot's advice to study under Koin of Mudera monastery (present-day Shiga Prefecture), but again found no satisfying answer. Koin referred him in turn to Eisai, who was at Kennin-ji temple in Kyoto and was known for his introduction of Rinzai Zen teachings from China.

When Dogen presented his problem to Eisai, the Rinzai master replied in koan-like fashion: "All the Buddhas in the three stages of time are unaware that they are endowed with the Buddha-nature, but cats and oxen are well aware of it indeed!" This was a kind of reversal of Joshu's koan: "Does a dog have Buddha-nature?" "Mu!" The suggestion that Buddhas do not think about their Buddha-nature, and that Dogen's problem is not a real problem for them, offered the first promise of a solution, and Dogen decided to study under Eisai.

When Eisai died the following year, Dogen continued his study and practice for nine years under Eisai's leading disciple, Myozen, and still searched for a definitive answer to his problem. At the age of twenty-three Dogen accompanied Myozen on a journey to China to visit some of the leading Ch'an monasteries. There he studied at Lin-chi (Rinzai) monasteries, first under Wu-chi of T'ien-t'ung Mountain, then under Ta-kuang of A-yu-wang Mountain, and finally under Che-weng of Ching Mountain. Two of these monasteries were of the Ta-hui branch of Lin-chi Zen, a branch which emphasized koan-meditation (*k'an-hua-ch'an*). It is no surprise that Dogen's writings frequently refer to koans, even though he was soon to turn to the silent-illumination zen (*me-chao-ch'an*) of the Ts'ao-tung School under the mentorship of Ju-ching (1163-1228).

For two years Dogen studied under the followers of the Ta-hui branch before attaching himself to Ju-ching. Dogen's opinion of the Lin-chi School, especially of Ta-hui and his teaching, was largely positive. Ta-hui had been the dominant exponent of Ch'an in 12th-century China and was noted for his interest in lay affairs and the education of a lay leadership in Buddhist principles. Three collections of his works contain his correspondence with 130 aristocrats and members of the gentry and contain advice, guidance, and criticism. His influence on Chinese society was greater than any Ch'an master before him, and he was unsurpassed in his monastic regimen and instruction. Like Hakuin six centuries later, Ta-hui was a staunch advocate of koan-introspection as the primary function of meditation, and was a critic of the "silent-illuminatiuon" approach of the Ts'ao-tung (Soto) School. He berated those who sat in silence and inaction, like inert blockheads, with eyes closed and minds empty. In his judgment the passivity and indecisiveness of silent-illumination Ch'an offered a gradualism that never arrived at the prize of enlightenment. It downplayed the importance of having a dramatic, definite, revolutionary experience of awakening, and satisfied itself with quietistic sitting. To him this was like "cold ash and dry wood." The koan-method, however, offered the possibility of a sudden breakthrough into a true understanding of the Dharma, a decisive and unforgettable moment of truth, and a radical transformation of one's consciousness.

Yet though Dogen studied for nine years in a Rinzai context in Japan and another two years in China, he found what for him was the authentic teacher in Ju-ching of the Ts'ao-tung School. During the early years after his return from China he did not speak critically of Ta-hui and his followers, presumbly because it was not a pressing issue. But later, when followers of Dainichibo joined Dogen's monastery in Fukakusa (1242), identifying themselves with the Ta-hui school, he became increasingly critical of Ta-hui's approach and understanding. He more sharply distinguished between Ta-hui and Ju-ching, and more firmly insisted on the authentic transmission of the Dharma through Ju-ching and the Ts'ao-tung School. "The document of succession of the Tung School is different from the Lin-chi School and other like schools. . . . It was only the monk Ch'ing-yuan who inherited the Seal of Approval [i.e., from the 6th Chinese Patriarch Hui-neng]. Other patriarchs do not measure up to him. Those who know this would know that the Buddha Dharma was authentically transmitted only to Ch'ing-yuan."[8] In another place Dogen says, "We cannot even say that Rinzai and Ummon have completely mastered the Buddhist Dharma."[9]

The originators of the Ts'ao-tung School in China were two monks of the late T'ang dynasty named Ts'ao-shan (840-901) and his master Tung-shan (807-869); from the hyphenation of these two names comes the Chinese name of the school (Ts'ao-tung) and hence the Japanese name (Soto). The two most significant figures prior to Ju-ching and Dogen, however, are Fu-yung (1043-1118) and Hung-chih (1091-1157). Fu-yung established high monastic ideals and rigorous practice, along with an emphasis upon frugality and simplicity. The latter was exemplified in his diet of rice and hot water, and his rejection of the offer of a purple robe from the Emperor. Hung-chih advocated silent-illumination meditation (Japanese, *mokushozen*) and was often criticized in this by his Lin-chi contemporary, Ta-hui. These emphases of Fu-yung and Hung-chih were combined in Ju-ching (and subsequently Dogen) who praised the monastic purity and simplicity of Fu-yung and commended Hung-chih's meditation manual, the *Tso-ch'an chen,* as superior to all others.

In Zen monastic tradition, monks were encouraged to move from monastery to monastery in order to perfect their understanding and to find the master who was right for their level of understanding and for their individual temperament. For Dogen, Ju-ching was the master for whom he had been searching. Writing in his journal, Dogen called the rare privilege he had of studying under Ju-ching "a blessing merited in a previous incarnation" (*Hokyo-ki,* sec. 1).

It was under Ju-ching that Dogen found a resolution to his central problem. During a period of meditation the monk next to Dogen had fallen asleep, and Ju-ching shouted at the sleeping monk: "In zazen you must cast off body and mind. How can you give in to single-minded intense sleeping?" The remark jolted Dogen into an understanding of the dilemmas he had been pondering, and he experienced a great sense of joy at his new-found discovery. There is no dualism of body and mind; no dualism of practice and enlightenment; no dualism of means and ends.

At first glance this scenario looks roughly parallel to that of Hakuin's early life and first enlightenment at twenty-four: a troubled soul searching for an answer, finding a solution, and experiencing liberation and joy. On closer examination, however, there are seen to be important differences. Dogen was not troubled in the same desperate and traumatic way as Hakuin, nor was he troubled with the same kind of problem. Dogen's problem was not some deep *internal* conflict issuing in emotional crises of doubt, depression, and guilt. It was more of an *external* problem about the traditional teachings of Mahayana Buddhism, a philosophical puzzle posed by an apparent contradiction in Mahayana doctrine and practice. That is to say, Dogen himself was not the problem. There is no suggestion of alienation from the Buddhist Way, of inner spiritual battles, or of anguish of soul. In searching for an answer to his questions he does not evidence a feeling of lostness, hopelessness, or condemnation. The issues do not seem to have tormented him, or driven him to the depths of melancholy and despair. He dealt with matters in what William James would have called a "healthy-minded" way: questioning, probing, testing, sifting, challenging, working through to a solution.

Unlike Hakuin, Dogen was not beset either by the condition of the sick-souled or the divided self. His belief in the efficacy of "single-minded intense sitting" is itself testimony to the absence of any significant sense of a divided self going in two opposite directions, or of the mental condition of the sick soul militating against the faith and determination which characterized Dogen's quest. Hakuin, to be sure, also talks about unrelenting resolve and advocates throwing one's total being into the koan. Yet this is, as it were, the *negative way*. It takes a condition of soul-sickness or divided self—or encourages the creation of one—and concentrates this condition in meditation on a koan; it brings the condition to a breaking point, after which may come new insight and resolution. Dogen's is the *positive way* which builds on a strong sense of naturalness, rightness, and goodness. Instead of beginning by concentrating on delusions and illusions, doubts and conflicts, and focussing them in a koan, Dogen's method is to concentrate upon faith in the fundamental purity and unity of one's nature.

In a sense, Dogen's "koan" was the very teaching and practice of Mahayana Buddhism itself, both in its Tendai and Rinzai forms. But the resolution at which Dogen arrives is not that of twice-born experience. The resolution that comes to him is that the religious practices of Buddhism are not means to the higher ends of Bodhi, Buddhahood, or Nirvana. The religious practices are *themselves* the goal of Buddhism. They are not means at all, but ends in themselves. Zazen—which for Dogen is the heart of Buddhist practice—is not a technique for searching after and gaining something. Nor is it a means of concentrating upon and struggling with the koan, which in turn can become the means to a breakthrough of insight. This would be

49

the equivalent of a means (zazen) to a means (koan introspection) to an end (enlightenment), which in turn is a means of achieving Buddhahood and Nirvana. For Dogen, sitting in meditation is to be practiced for its own sake. This is, so to speak, the way Buddhas sit.

Similarly, the aim is not to obtain a radical alteration of one's thought and perception. Rather, there is no aim at all. If one's original nature is enlightened, is Buddha, then there is nothing for which to seek, nothing to gain. This is what one is most fundamentally. To seek for what one already has is like—in the words of Po-chang—"riding the ox in search of the ox." The reference is to the ox-herding parable in which a farmer, who thinks he has lost his ox, mounts his ox and rides off searching the countryside for it. To use a modern analogy, searching for Bodhi, Buddhahood, and Nirvana is like searching for one's glasses while wearing one's glasses. If such a search is to be brought to a successful conclusion, it can only be by putting a stop to the search. This, for Dogen, is the most literal understanding of *kensho*, "seeing into one's own nature." And it is in full accord with the ancient Ch'an and Taoist principles of no-seeking (*wu-chin*) and non-action (*wu-wei*).

This "attainment which is no-attainment" that Dogen realized in China was expressed in humorous fashion after his return. At the opening ceremonies for a meditation hall which Dogen had constructed, he commented on what he had learned from his experiences and studies abroad: "I realized clearly that my eyes are set horizontally and my nose vertically. I returned to Japan without carrying a single sutra. So I have no Buddhism to offer."

Dogen's Alleged "Great Doubt" and Satori

In 1253, following the death of Dogen, his leading disciple Ejo discovered the journal which Dogen had kept (the *Hokyo-ki*), a journal which was apparently never intended for publication. Dogen kept it to preserve the words of the esteemed master for his own personal use and for guidance in his instruction of his own disciples. It recorded the responses which the master Ju-ching had made to Dogen's questions and the instructions which he had given during the period 1225-27. It is clear from the journal that Dogen had a very questioning mind, and that he had a great many questions. While one issue has been singled out by interpreters as the central and burning issue for Dogen, and compared with Hakuin's Great Doubt, it is but one among a great variety of questions Dogen raised. And if a general characterization were to be given to the questions, it would have to be that they were not motivated by doubt or despair but by faith seeking understanding. They were eager questions, not desperate ones.

Dogen's first recorded question had to do with the correctness of the Zen teaching concerning the transmission of the Dharma outside the scriptures. Ju-ching's response was to reaffirm the transmission outside the scriptures (i.e. experiencing the truth through meditation under an authentic master), but not so as to discount the importance of the scriptural teachings of the Buddha. As Ju-ching insisted in a later dialogue, "Both sacred silence and sacred teaching are the undertakings of the Buddha."[10]

Dogen's second question had to do with the issue of questions and answers themselves. Citing the familiar Zen themes of the wordlessness of the Dharma and its unmediated experience, Dogen asked whether the non-verbal techniques for which Zen masters were noted were in accord with the Way of the Buddhas and Patriarchs. "The masters raise their fists or lift up a fly whisk, shout loudly or give a blow with a stick. They do not bother to explain to their students what they mean. Neither do they allow them to inquire how the Buddhas convert people."[11] The clear indication of the question, and of the many recorded dialogues between Dogen and Ju-ching, is that, while Ju-ching resolutely advocated silent meditation and did not use the *nembutsu* or koan meditation, he nevertheless encouraged sincere questions and gave careful answers. In fact, the *Hokyo-ki* begins by noting that "even if he [Dogen] was untimely and not properly dressed, what this lowly man from a far-away foreign country wanted most was to visit the Abbot's quarters frequently and ask questions, however audacious they might be."[12]

Dogen then reports how Ju-ching, in his compassion and sympathy, "pitied Dogen and allowed him to be heard as he sought the Way and the Dharma." Indeed, Ju-ching encouraged Dogen to come to him at any time to air his questions. "Dogen, you must seek instruction from now on, whether during the day or night, whether clad in a formal monk's robe or not. Come to the Abbot's quarters without reservation to inquire in the Way. I will always forgive your lack of propriety, as would a father."[13] Dogen eagerly and happily

51

took up the rare invitation and came thereafter with what must have seemed like an endless stream of questions. Like any great teacher, Ju-ching was likewise delighted with a student who not only had many questions, but penetrating and profound ones. On one occasion Ju-ching exclaimed, "It is excellent that you ask this question. No one has ever asked this question, and therefore no one else knows the answer. This is what the good teachers suffer. When I was at the late Master's monastery on Hsueh-tou Mountain, I asked this question and the late Master was immensely pleased."[14]

The supposed "Great Doubt" of Dogen, and the attempt to fit him into the pattern of Rinzai experience, is not borne out by Dogen's own journal. His question concerning original and acquired enlightenment, though a major issue for him (as it was for Mahayana Buddhism generally at the time), was but one among many questions of considerable variety, from the nature of the Dharma to monks' robes. The questions, furthermore, are those of a brilliant and inquiring mind, full of energy and fascination, like a child set loose in a wonderland, asking "What?" and "Why?" about everything.

Some questions puzzled Dogen over a longer period than others, and were not as easily resolved. The original/acquired enlightenment issue was one of these, and certainly was a central issue. Yet Dogen did not treat the issue as a koan, or turn it into a koan, or see it as a means of intensifying doubt, or understand it as a condensation and consequence of false and illusory ways of thinking. Nor are the answers at which he arrived the product of some sudden enlightenment in the sense of a satori. Perhaps the resolutions which he periodically experienced may be spoken of as a species of *kensho*, of seeing into his inner nature, but they do not appear to involve the kinds of dramatic experiences which Hakuin reports.

Takashi Kodera repeatedly refers to this set of issues as Dogen's "Great Doubt." But this is quite misleading, and is an interpretation of Dogen's experience in terms of Hakuin's twice-born experience, and of Dogen's understanding in terms of the teachings and methods of a Rinzai master. Dogen after all did *not* find satisfactory answers to his many questions during his nine years of Rinzai study in Japan and his two years of further Rinzai (Lin-chi) study in China. It was only under Ju-ching that he received answers that he found helpful and acceptable—and they were largely in the form of verbal answers to questions posed, not koanic insights arrived at through the collapse of question and answer. As we have seen, Ju-ching said that they were excellent questions, questions that needed to be asked, questions that less motivated and perceptive monks were not asking. And clearly Dogen found in Ju-ching's responses excellent answers.

One of the reasons for Dogen's long period of questioning on so many issues is not at all that he was a "doubting Thomas" type but that he was a curious and questioning type. He was not impressed with the state of Buddhism in Japan, and did not have full confidence in any Japanese master. Since Japanese Buddhism was so dependent upon Chinese Buddhism, it was only natural for him to widen the horizon of his quest and eventually go to China to study. He deeply desired to find a master whose teachings could, with full confidence, be said to be authentic and whose whole-hearted commitment to the Way of the Buddha was unmistakable. Frequently in his writings Dogen laments the confused and degenerate state of Buddhism in his time—to that extent giving credence to the Degenerate Age teaching of other sects. For him, however, this was not an inevitability of history. He was dedicated to recovering and restoring the most authentic and committed Buddhism. If, then, Dogen had any "Great Doubt" it was doubt about the authenticity and commitment of much of the Buddhism of his day. It was not motivated by doubt about Buddhism or about himself. It was not Hakuin's "existential doubt" but an empirical doubt; he doubted much of what he saw and heard.

Quite consistent with this, Dogen never made Great Doubt a precondition of enlightenment, nor did he employ any devices—whether koan, shouting, striking, etc.—to encourage it, develop it, or bring it to a climax. For Dogen the opposite, if anything, was the case. What was of critical importance to him was Great Faith, faith in the existence of an authentic teaching, authentic teachers, the unsurpassed example of the Buddha, an unbroken line of transmission of the Buddha Dharma, and one's inherent Buddha-nature. Dogen would not have subscribed to the suggestion that doubt precedes enlightenment, or that the greater the precedent doubt the greater the enlightenment. For Dogen faith is fundamental, and faith is itself an expression of one's Buddha-nature and intrinsic enlightenment.

It is not only alleged by those who would interpret Dogen's experience and teaching in Rinzai terms that he wrestled for years with the "koan" of original/acquired enlightenment and was plunged into a "Great Doubt" over the matter. It is also alleged that Dogen finally experienced a Rinzai-like satori during the aforementioned episode in which Ju-ching shouted at a sleeping monk, jolting Dogen into a realization of the issues he had been pondering. What is critical in this episode is not Dogen's sense of delight in newfound understanding—natural enough relative to any quandary over which one might ponder for some time. It is the phrasing of Ju-ching's reprimand of the sleeping monk that is critical: "In zazen you must cast off body and mind. How can you give in to single-minded intense *sleeping?*" What is commonly missed here is that the phrase "single-minded intense *sitting*" was central in the teaching of Ju-ching, and that Ju-ching was making a pun. The pun indicated by the italics is apparently what helped trigger Dogen's understanding.

One implication of the pun is that in "single-minded intense *sleeping*" the dualistic concepts of body and mind are dropped in unconsciousness and the weary sleeper has given himself over entirely, "body and soul," to sleep. In sleep there is no distinction, no duality between body and mind. But there is no consciousness either. "Single-minded intense sitting" (*chih-kuan ta-tso*, Japanese *shikantaza*) is analogous to the state of the sleeper, only in heightened consciousness rather than unconsciousness. If one sat in the same totality and unity of body-mind as this monk in deep sleep, one would be sitting squarely within the Buddha Dharma.

On this realization Dogen builds his own radical emphasis upon *shikantaza* and his interpretation of *shikantaza* as an end—sitting within one's enlightenment and Buddha-nature—rather than a means to enlightenment and Buddhahood. Dogen comments on this episode in the *Shobogenzo:* "Through the dropping of body and mind I received the face-to-face transmission, and thence I returned to Japan."[15] When Dogen reported his insight to Ju-ching, he gave Dogen his seal of approval, saying, "You have indeed dropped body and mind."[16]

The two phrases—"dropping body and mind" and "single-minded intense sitting"—provided a solution to the persistent quandary concerning original and acquired enlightenment. The two phrases are like the two sides of the same coin. "Single-minded intense sitting" *is* the dropping of body and mind. And to sit in that state is to sit within one's original nature. "Single-minded intense sitting" and "dropping body and mind" are the manifestation and confirmation of one's original nature. They are not an acquisition, since they represent one's most fundamental state of being.

CHAPTER IV

A Philosophy of Buddhist Confirmation

*Do not think that you will necessarily be aware of
your own enlightenment.*

Shunryu Suzuki

If the Zen of Rinzai and Hakuin stresses the twice-born experience
of a "sudden enlightenment," perhaps the once-born Zen of Ju-ching
and Dogen fosters a "gradual enlightenment" approach—a position
that was decisively rejected in the early history of Ch'an. Dogen,
however, argues that his position is the more thoroughgoing sudden
enlightenment teaching; for what could be more sudden than to accept
one's enlightenment and Buddha-nature from the beginning of one's
practice, and to see one's practice as an expression of that original
Buddhahood? On the other hand, Rinzai/Hakuin Zen, for all its
emphasis upon and attempts to foster an experience of sudden
enlightenment, is seen as having the look of gradualism about it; for
one is given a koan with which to wrestle and is goaded by various
proddings, all in the expectation of achieving a satori after several
weeks, months, years. And after the first koan is "solved" one is
then given another to work on, and so on *ad infinitum*.

Dogen's *Fukan zazen-gi* (General Recommendations for Sitting
Meditation) contains a succinct statement of the position at which he
had arrived. "Do not sit in order to become a Buddha," he warns,
"because that has nothing to do with such things as sitting or lying
down."[1] The essay was originally drafted by Dogen at the age of
twenty-eight after returning from China. And it was several times

reworked, indicating the importance he attached to its content and phrasing.

> The Way is essentially perfect and exists everywhere. There is no need either to seek or to realize the Way. The Truth which carries us along is sovereign and does not require our efforts. . . Essentially the Truth is very close to you; is it then necessary to run around in search of it?. . . That which we call *zazen* is not a way of developing concentration. It is simply the comfortable way. It is practice which measures your enlightenment to the fullest, and is in fact enlightenment itself. It is the manifestation of the ultimate reality. . .[2]

Dogen thus rejects the common suggestion of a hope or expectation that seeks something in the future, or in some other life, or in eternity—anywhere outside the present moment. One does not have to strive to reach at long last the far horizon of nirvana; one need only allow one's primordial nirvana-mind to come to bear on the present moment. The same understanding may be seen preserved 700 years later in the words of a contemporary Soto master, Taizan Maezumi: "The point of our practice is not to become something other than what we already are. . . [but to] become aware of the fact that we are intrinsically, originally the Way itself, which is free and complete."[3]

The Practice of Healthy-Mindedness

In this one sees a religious understanding which is on the order of what William James characterizes as the healthy-minded, once-born perspective. One is not fundamentally sick, but healthy; not sinful, but pure; not broken, but whole; not in bondage, but free; not in error, but in the truth. There are some persons, wrote James, who are "born with an inner constitution which is harmonious and well-balanced from the outset. Their impulses are consistent with one another, their will follows without trouble the guidance of their intellect, their passions are not excessive, and their lives are little haunted by regrets."[4] For them goodness is conceived as the central and all-embracing aspect of being. Instead of dwelling on the evils and woes of the world, they emphasize the "dignity rather than the depravity of man."[5] There is no felt need for a "radical reconstitution of the psyche or world, for we are already one with the Divine without any miracle of grace, or abrupt creation of a new inner man."[6]

Dogen insists that all have "the seed of realizing Buddhahood,"[7] and that "even an insight as small as a speck of dust will ultimately give us right understanding."[8] The watchwords, therefore, are not conversion and rebirth, but faith and confirmation; not death and resurrection, but growth and maturation. The emphasis, correspondingly, is not on an eradication of one's deluded and evil inclinations, nor the fostering of doubt concerning all that one is and thinks and presupposes, but the nurture of one's natural propensities to goodness and harmony.

As in those Christian communions that mark entrance into the faith and life of the Church in infancy through the sacrament of baptism, as distingished from those that insist on a personal conversion in early adulthood and public confession through believer's baptism, the issue is not one of regeneration but confirmation. One is nurtured in a faith and practice that continues to confirm itself. In the *Gakudo yojin-shu* (Points to Watch in Buddhist Training) Dogen uses the analogy of animals rearing their young. In the same manner, the various Buddhas in their compassion are said to nurture those who are "the children of the Buddha," aiding them to grow and develop in their practice of the Buddhist Way. The Buddhist practitioner begins in that faith, which repeatedly is confirmed in practice. Dogen in fact often used the term *sho* (confirmation, authentication) rather than *satori* or *kaku* (awakening).

The 9th-century master Tai-chu (Daishu) once exclaimed, in terms anticipating those of Dogen: "No bondage from the first, and what is the use of seeking emancipation? Act as you will, go on as you feel—without a second thought. This is the incomparable way."[9] Dogen insists that we are never aliens relative to the way of the Buddha but are already, from the beginning, children of the Buddha. Even more sweepingly he states that "in the entire universe there is not a single object alien from the Buddha-nature." Thus, as one engages in zazen, "irrespective of intelligence, he will mature naturally."[10] The task is not to seek to become something other than we already are, but to allow our Buddha-nature to manifest and realize itself (*genjo*) and thus to be confirmed (*sho*) in the Dharma.

To those who are seeking ecstatic experiences and sudden transformations, Dogen says "they are like a child who, forsaking his father and his father's wealth, runs away from home. Even though his father is rich, and he, as an only son, will someday inherit it all, he becomes a beggar, searching for his fortune in faraway places."[11] Dogen's prodigal son seeks elsewhere, that is, for the birthright that is already his and the home that he need only claim.

For Dogen, therefore, one must engage in zazen—and all other activities—with a non-seeking mind, first because what one seeks for one already is, and secondly because no-striving and no-desiring is the essence of the Way and the estate of one's true and original being. To strive for something which one desires for oneself is in contradiction to the announced objective of one's seeking and desiring, namely the state of no-striving, no-desiring, and no-self. In Dogen's *Fukan zagen-gi* it is stressed from the outset that "it is unnecessary to distinguish between 'practice' and 'enlightenment'. The supreme teaching is free, so why study the means to attain it? The Way is, needless to say, very far from delusion. Why, then, be concerned about the means of eliminating the latter? The Way is completely present where you are, so of what use is practice or enlightenment?"[12]

To seek enlightenment and the truth which enlightenment bestows is to separate yourself from enlightenment and the truth. For the enlightened state is the state of no-seeking and no-striving, which is one's intrinsic state. Thus Dogen remarks in the *Gengokoan* fascicle: "At first, when you seek the truth, you have distanced yourself from its domain. Finally, when the truth is correctly transmitted to you, you are immediately the primordial person."[13] This "primordial person" (*honbunnin*) is one's Buddha-nature, or, in Hui-neng's words, "Your original face before you were born."

As T.P. Kasulis has phrased the issue, "To say that one practices zazen in order to become an enlightened person is like saying one practices medicine to become a doctor. To practice medicine is to *be* a doctor. To practice zazen is to *be* enlightened. Enlightenment is not a static state of achievement; it is the active undertaking of the Way exemplified in zazen."[14] In zazen one sits within the non-reflective state of no-thought and no-desire, to which Dogen refers by the term *hishiryo* (without-thinking) or the traditional term *mushin* (no-mind). If one spends one's life meditating upon koans, one is rarely in that state, for thought and effort are constantly riveted upon a koan, presumably in order to project oneself into the state of no-mindedness, yet spending the majority of one's time and energy living outside that state.

Enlightenment for Dogen, then, is not an event, or series of events, brought about by koan-introspection in which the light suddenly strikes one who otherwise sits in darkness, but rather is the light within which one sits, lives, and moves, and has one's being. One should not speak of "being enlightened" but of "enlightened being." Being enlightened suggests an achievement or a movement from one house to another. Enlightened being is one's true home and state of being.

This is not to say that there are no distinctions to be made between spiritual masters and the novice monk of a day, or between Buddhas and ne'er-do-wells. When Dogen asked Ju-ching whether it was correct to say that all sentient beings were authentically awakened Buddhas, Ju-ching replied: "Saying that sentient beings are originally Buddhas is the same as believing the heterodoxy of spontaneous origination [rather than 'dependent origination']. We cannot condone those who compare 'I' and 'mine' with the Buddhas, and who take the unattained as the attained and the unexperienced as the experienced."[15]

Later in the *Bendowa* Dogen addresses the issue by saying, "all are fully endowed with it [the Buddha-nature], but while there is no practice it is not manifest, and while it is not realized there is no attainment."[16] Here we find a distinction reminiscent of the Aristotelean distinction between potential and actual. Everyone has the potential for full understanding, but unless put into practice and individually realized, it does not become actualized. It is as if to say that everyone is endowed with spiritual muscles, but those muscles must be used. They must be exercised, developed, employed.

In discussing the importance of an authentic teacher in the *Gaduko yojin-shu*, Dogen uses the analogy of the craftsman and his material. The aspiring student is like the block of wood which has the potential for becoming a fine carving in the hands of a master carver. Even the finest material cannot be carved into a finished piece without the aid of a good craftsman. Dogen accordingly rejects the notion of "spontaneous realization"—i.e., without dependence upon others who

61

have realized the Way of the Buddha and stand in historical continuity with him. Having access to authentic teaching in unbroken transmission from the time of the Buddha is essential. To abandon this principle is to violate the Buddhist doctrine of dependent origination. The Way of the Buddha is a lived experience, transmitted and reaffirmed from person to person. The Truth, the Way, is already within each person, but it must be brought forth into realization and manifestation. "All Buddhas, Mahasattvas, and sentient beings clarify the Great Way of *dharmata* through the power of innate knowledge. Following the sutras or masters and clarifying the Great Way of *dharmata* is the illumination of one's own knowledge."[17]

From Enlightenment to Meditation

The early life of the Buddha would seem to be the most supportive of a twice-born Zen, and is so understood by the Rinzai sect. The interpretation usually given of the Buddha-story is that Gautama, disenchanted with palace life and disillusioned over the sights of old age, disease and death, searched in vain for six years for peace of mind, nearly starving himself to death in his determined quest, but finally winning through to enlightenment after a series of titanic struggles under the Bodhi tree. That is certainly the interpretation used to the full by Hakuin. Yet Dogen has his own reading which is in accord with his once-born type of religious experience and understanding. The six years in the wilderness are not seen as the Buddha's searching for enlightenment, but as the expression of his pre-existent Dharma. In Dogen's basic guide to meditation, the *Fukan zazengi,* he speaks of the Buddha as one "who saw all things as they truly are with his own enlightened nature, and yet still did zazen for six years."[18]

This understanding is seen by Dogen as receiving additional confirmation from the case of Bodhidharma, reputedly the first to bring Zen practice from India to China. Upon arriving in China, Bodhidharma did not actively pursue missionary work from place to place, but instead went into the mountains and meditated for nine years facing the wall of a cave. If Bodhidharma was meditating for nine years in search of enlightenment, what wisdom was he bringing from India? And why would he come all the way from India in search of something that originated in India? In Dogen's view, therefore,

Bodhidharma's meditation must not be seen as the way *to* enlightenment but the way *of* enlightenment. Bodhidharma's meditation facing the wall for nine years was not a prelude to his awakening or a preparation for his missionary work. This *was* his message and his transmission of Bodhi and Dharma.

In this manner Dogen reversed the traditional sequence of morality, meditation, and enlightenment. It had been commonly understood that observance of the moral precepts of the Buddha was the precondition of proper meditational practice, which was in turn the precondition of enlightenment. Yet such a movement would only reinforce the very problems from which, presumably, enlightenment brings deliverance: self-seeking, desire, attachment, and the dualistic separation of experience into subject and object, means and ends, present and future, not-having and having. Further, Dogen asks, if one meditates and engages in moral purification for many years for the sake of achieving the experience of enlightenment, for what purpose would one continue meditation and moral purification *after* this experience?

Dogen resolves the difficulty by giving an opposite order to the traditional sequence. Enlightenment is the basis of morality and meditation, these two forms being the natural expression of enlightenment. Enlightenment is not the goal of one's effort, but its point of departure. Thus one should not "anticipate a realization apart from practice, because practice points directly to original realization."[19] It is none other than "the enlightened mind which arouses the thought of enlightenment."[20] Most simply put, this is to say that "only Buddhas can become Buddhas" (*yuibutsu jobutsu*). In the same fashion Dogen argues that the traditional scheme of the Thirty-Seven Stages Toward Enlightenment should not be understood as stations along a path but as the thirty-seven virtues *of* enlightenment. In the *Fukan zazen-gi* Dogen insists that "zazen is not 'step-by-step meditation'. Rather it is simply the easy and pleasant practice of a Buddha, the manifestation of the Buddha's Wisdom. The Truth appears, there being no delusion."[21]

If zazen (or koan-zen) is the means to enlightenment, why did the Buddha practice zazen for fifty more years after his experiences under the Bodhi tree? Dogen responds by distinguishing between meditation for its own sake (*jijuyu*) and meditation for the sake of something else (*tajuyu*). Meditation in its purity is not a means to an end but an enjoyment of one's own Dharma-nature. Its value is not instrumental; it is the self-enjoyment of a Buddha. The proper answer to the question as to why one continues to engage in zazen is that this is the natural posture and activity of a Buddha.

> Very foolish people think that when we study Buddhism we do not arrive at the Buddhist Way until our study is completed. This occurs because such people do not know that proclaiming, practicing, and enlightening the Buddhist Way are all complete within themselves and contain all aspects of the Way. They say that only those who are lost in illusion need to practice the Buddhist Way and attain great enlightenment. They do not know that even those who are not in illusion practice the Buddhist Way diligently.[22]

An analogy may be drawn from painting. One may paint for a living, or as a discharge of inner tensions and conflicts, as in using art as therapy. But one may also paint as a natural expression of one's inner harmony, and because one enjoys painting. Painting for the sake of painting is the highest level of art, for its object is itself in the present moment of activity and not some goal outside itself in some future moment. Likewise, painting as an expression of inner harmony, or of one's harmony with the subject being painted and the season (two basic principles of Zen art), is a higher level of art than painting as an expression of inner tensions, or of conflicts with others. While Rinzai Zen uses zazen and the koan to focus inner tensions and outer conflicts in order to bring these disharmonies to a breaking point, Dogen is insistent that zazen is properly the expression of inner harmony and tranquillity.

A favorite phrase of Dogen's was *honsho myoshu*, the "wonderful practice of intrinsic enlightenment." In his treatise on monastic training (*Gaduko yojin-shu*) he admonishes: "Do not practice Buddhism for your own benefit, for fame and profit, or for rewards and miraculous powers. Simply practice Buddhism for the sake of Buddhism; this is the Way." Or again, "For playing joyfully in *samadhi* the upright sitting in meditation is the right gate."[23]

It is true that Dogen and other Soto masters before and after him have collected koans and occasionally referred to them or used them in their teaching. The use of the koan in Soto, however, is more as an expression of one's understanding (when used by the disciple), or as a seal of approval on one's understanding (when used by the master). The koan is, in this context, the paradoxical articulation of the Dharma and one's insight into the Dharma. In Rinzai, on the other hand, the koan is used as a device for precipitating understanding, and once a particular koan becomes a vehicle of insight, another koan is assigned for meditation and resolution. Thus again, we observe a familiar difference in pattern. In Rinzai the koan moves *toward* insight; in Soto it proceeds *from* insight.

A common image of Buddhist practice and aspiration in the history of Buddhism is that of crossing the river from the present shore of samsara to the "other shore" of nirvana. The raft which one uses to cross to the other side is provided by the teachings of the Buddha and Patriarchs, and by means of their guidance and one's resolute spiritual practices one may pole across the turbulent current to the distant shore. Relative to that familiar image and phrasing Dogen says, "*Paramita* means 'gone to the other shore'. The other shore is not originally characterized by coming and going. . . . Do not think that we arrive at the other shore after practice. We have practice on the other shore and therefore arrive there."[24]

Beyond Dualism

While in Rinzai koan-meditation is the means whereby one aims to frustrate dualistic thinking and transcend the discriminating mind, in Dogen's understanding zazen itself is that state of being in which one sits outside of all dualisms and discriminating thought. This was the understanding to which Dogen came on hearing Ju-ching's words to the sleeping monk. Thus, he says that in zazen "your body and mind will naturally fall away, and your original Buddha-nature will appear. . . By virtue of zazen it is possible to transcend the difference between 'common' and 'sacred'. . . . Zazen is a practice beyond the subjective and objective worlds, beyond discriminating thinking."[25]

In the Buddhist tradition meditation and wisdom have often been seen as the twin pillars of the Dharma. Much earlier the Sixth Chinese Patriarch, Hui-neng, had argued that meditation (*ting*) should not be separated from wisdom (*hui*). In his remarkable *Platform Sutra* Hui-neng taught that they were "a unity, not two things. Meditation

65

itself is the substance of wisdom; wisdom itself is the function of meditation. Students, be careful not to say that meditation gives rise to wisdom, or that wisdom gives rise to meditation, or that meditation and wisdom are different from each other. To hold this view implies that things have duality.''[26] Dualism is one of the basic issues in Zen, which sees itself as fundamentally non-dualistic. Dogen clearly shares this same concern to define meditation and wisdom in their inseparable unity (*shusho itto*), and to avoid all misleading and confounding dualisms: practice and enlightenment, means and ends, present and future, subject and object, mind and body, faith and life.

A particularly crucial problem of dualism stressed by Dogen is that of the separation of life into religious and secular, sacred and profane, significant and trivial. In the *Bendowa* (Practice of the Way) section of the *Shobogenzo* Dogen rejects the common distinction between spiritual and worldly affairs, as if certain human activities such as meditating, keeping monastic precepts, sutra-chanting, studying Buddhist texts, etc., were holier and more important enterprises than cooking, sweeping, gardening, or gathering wood. Dogen clearly stands in the tradition of many Zen defenders of the commonplace and the everyday, such as Ch'ang-ch'ing ("Come, let us have a cup of tea"), Yun-men ("Pulling a plough in the morning, carrying a rake home in the evening"), and P'ang Chu-shih ("How wonderous is this, how marvellous! I carry fuel, I draw water.").

Dogen insists that "there is nothing such as worldly affairs to be distinguished from the Way." In the *Senjo* section he argues that the so-called "majestic activities" of the Buddhas and Patriarchs are not to be separated from or elevated above supposedly inferior activities. The way in which one performs daily tasks (*samu*), the manner in which one washes face and hands, even one's comportment in the latrine, are all equally important as the "majestic activities." Dogen at one point boldly declares: "The Buddha finds an opportunity to turn the wheel of Dharma in the latrine!" Nothing stands outside the Way of the Buddha, and within the Way there is no duality of superior and inferior, sacred and profane.

Again we have a position characteristic of the once-born, healthy-minded type. A contemporary Soto master, Abbot Obora, expresses Dogen's position in this way: "Our Buddhism has to be manifest in every movement of the hand and every pace of the foot. Taking up the food must be with the firmness of establishing a mighty temple, lifting and lowering the chopsticks must be with the power which turns the wheel of the Law. Not in great matters alone is there to be the great manifestation—in the tiniest thing we must grasp the power which pervades the universe."[27]

When Dogen had visited China as a young monk, an event occurred which had a profound influence on his subsequent thinking about such matters, and which probably had much to do with his finding a solution shortly thereafter to the various dualisms that had been concerning him. Dogen had remained quartered on ship for several months, during which time the ship was visited by an older Zen monk who was chief cook in a monastery some 85 miles away. The old monk had come to purchase mushrooms for his kitchen. Dogen invited him to stay overnight on board, but the monk declined, saying that he needed to return to his duties as soon as possible. Dogen expressed surprise that others could not carry on such menial tasks, and that a senior monk should still be burdened with kitchen duties rather than be free to meditate and engage in other religious practices. The monk laughed and said, "Perhaps you do not understand the practice of the Way, or what words and letters are." The exchange awakened Dogen to the realization that the distinctions between "religious" and "secular," and between "edifying" and "menial," are illusory distinctions—"words and letters" which divide and discriminate.

It is noteworthy that shortly after Dogen founded his own monastic center Eiheiji (1244), he wrote works such as *Eiheiji jikuimmon* which exalted the significance of preparing and eating meals, and *Fushukuhampo*, which interpreted the eating of food as itself a partaking of the Dharma of the Buddha. And where but in Zen would one find a book like Dogen's *Tenzo kyokun* (Instructions to the Kitchen Supervisor)? In this work Dogen describes at length his encounter with the Chinese monastery cook, indicating the profound effect that brief meeting had on his understanding of Zen practice.

Dogen had travelled to China in the hope of learning the authentic Zen teaching and practice first-hand. At one point in his discussion with the old cook, the cook said, "To study words is to understand the origin of words; to engage in discipline is to probe the origin of discipline."[28] The key term in both statements is "origin." Words do not lead toward understanding but proceed from it; discipline does not achieve a foreign goal but receives its impetus from one's original nature. One does not realize understanding or purify practice by reducing the amount of time spent on secular activities, such as cooking, and increasing the amounts of time spent on meditation, chanting, the study of sutras, etc. All activities engaged in with one's Buddha-mind are enlightened activities and the Way of the Buddha.

Following the Zen custom he had encountered in China, Dogen placed the chief cook among the six highest officers (*chiji*) in the monastery, a position previously unheard of in Japanese monasticism. Monks were taught to speak honorifically of the plainest foods: *on-kayu* (honorable gruel), *on-toki* (honorable rice), *on-shiru* (honorable soup). Ordinary objects, such as the monk's bowl, are referred to as "miraculous utensils" (*kidoku no chodo*), and their use in eating is a "miraculous event" (*kidoku no koto*). Dogen even devised a chant to be used in conjunction with tooth-brushing:

> Using the wooden tooth-brush each morning,
> May I vow with sentient beings
> To attain teeth strong enough
> To gnaw on all illusions.[29]

In a similar manner Dogen challenges the distinction made in the Jodo-shin sect of Buddhism between the Pure Land (*jodo*) of Amida's Western Paradise and the Defiled Land (*edo*) of this world of samsara in this degenerate age (*mappo*). Purity and peace and Buddhahood are to be found in *this* world, in this *present* age, in this *moment* of time, within *oneself*. The "Pure Land" is to be found within this "Defiled Land."

Dogen likewise rejected the dualistic understanding of nirvana and samsara. "To enter nirvana is to enter our clenched fist [the actions of everyday life] and carry on our natural life."[30] The cycle of birth and death is not to be denigrated as evil or looked upon as a process to be negated and transcended. It is to be seen as a marvelous opportunity. Nirvana, on the other hand, is not to be viewed as a state beyond and outside of samsara, to be attained through some method of escape from this world. The state of nirvana is a way of living in the world of samsara. "Just understand that birth and death itself is nirvana, and you will neither hate the one as being birth and death, nor cherish the other as being nirvana. Only then can you be free of birth and death. . . . This present birth and death itself is the life of Buddha. If you attempt to reject it with distaste, you are losing thereby the life of Buddha. . . . You only attain the mind of Buddha when there is no hating and no desiring.''[31]

This perspective is further expanded by identifying the Buddha-nature with the impermanence of all things (*mujo*). Buddha-nature is not one thing (permanence) and the impermanence of samsara another. "Impermanence *is* Buddha-nature" (*mujo-bussho*). The impermanence of life has, of course, been a basic teaching of Buddhism from its inception. But often this has been interpreted by contrasting the transciency and restless movement of this world with the permanence and imperturbability of the eternal realm of nirvana. Dogen counters this dualism by insisting that the impermanence of all things is itself the Buddha-nature. The realization and acceptance of this fact is the manifestation of enlightenment. And neither despising nor clinging to this world of samsara is the liberation and peace of nirvana.

Buddha-nature, too, is not to be understood as nature in the sense of permanent substance. It is not some eternal substratum which, like the depths of the ocean, remains unchanging while everything else changes like tossing waves on the surface—a position to which Indian mysticism has been inclined. Buddha-nature is to be understood as emptiness (*sunyata*). "Since the Buddha-nature is empty, it is called *mu* (no-thing)."[32] The Buddha-nature is not a some*thing* which is *possessed* by beings. The common reading of the passage in the *Nirvana Sutra*, "All living beings *have* the Buddha nature," was accordingly retranslated by Dogen to read, "All beings *are* the Buddha nature." Buddha-nature is not an object of possession, nor can it be made an object of acquisition. It is the fundamental, pure and free, universal emptiness of all things.

The result of all this is that Dogen also criticizes a mind/body, spirit/matter dualism. The function of moral and meditational practice is not to develop the control of the mind over the body, or to emanicipate spirit from flesh, or to be transported in enlightenment out of the world of maya. Mind or spirit is not the vehicle through which one hopes eventually to escape from the body, matter, or world as "the prisonhouse of the soul," as in the dualisms of Samkhya Yoga,

Vedanta, and the Platonists. The distinctions between mind/body, spirit/flesh, eternity/time, changeless/changing, nirvana/samsara, are the very dualisms from which one is to be delivered. *This* is maya: the illusions and delusions created by dualistic thinking.

Thus Dogen argues that the terms *zazen* and *shikantaza* do not refer only to a physical posture through which one attempts to realize a mental state of spiritual experience. They refer to a non-dualistic state of "sitting," in which these very dualisms do not exist. One is to "just sit," not only in the literal posture of zazen, but in everything that one does. This is the full meaning of "to cast off mind and body." Distinctions between mind and body, spirit and flesh, sacred and profane, significant and trivial, are *abstractions* from what is fundamentally one reality. In that one reality, and out of that one reality—which is fundamentally true, good, pure, and free—one "sits," that is, one resides.

Similarly, scripture for Dogen is not to be separated, packaged, labelled, and set apart from the world or from the common, ordinary acts of life. The sutras do not consist only of the holy words of Sakyamuni Buddha or other Buddhas, set down in this or that text, to be studied in splendid isolation. The words of the Buddha may be found everywhere and in all things. "This 'sutra' is the sutra of the entire universe—mountains, rivers, earth, grass, trees, self, and others. It is the taking of meals and the wearing of clothes, the work of everyday life."[33]

CHAPTER V

The Log-Jam and the Muddy Pond

The contrasts between the biographies and teachings of Hakuin and Dogen leave us with a major issue in understanding the Zen tradition. Do the once-born and twice-born kinds of religious experience and interpretation lead to radically different forms of Zen? When one examines the actual consequences of these different readings of Zen experience, they *do* seem considerable in the areas of Zen training and pedagogical technique, and in the respective experiences and understandings of Zen that accompany these. Given the centrality of meditation in Zen, not only during the specific hours of meditation and the intensive periods of meditation (*sesshin*) but as a meditative state within which one is to live every waking moment, these differences would seem to affect the whole of the Zen life.

Commonalities

At the same time, important commonalities must be noted. Rinzai as well as Soto claims to be non-dualist, the *satori* experience itself being one in which dualistic modes of thinking and perceiving are seen as collapsed and transcended. On the other hand, even though Dogen relentlessly attacks dualisms of many sorts, including those which the Rinzai sect seems to foster, some distinctions must still be acknowledged along the way, such as between those who are aware of their Buddha-nature and those who are not, those who have correct teaching and practice and those who do not, those who are masters and those who are novices, etc. It was Dogen who said, "Although

71

the Dharma is amply present in every person, unless one practices, it is not manifested; unless there is realization, it is not attained."[1]

Rinzai as well as Soto agrees that one's original nature is pure and enlightened, only needing to be awakened from the depths of one's being. Hakuin, for example, insists that "Man is endowed with the wisdom and form of the Buddha. There is nothing that he lacks. Each person is endowed with this treasure jewel that is the Buddha-nature."[2] Hakuin's *Zazen Wasan* (Chant in Praise of Zazen), which is commonly chanted in Rinzai monasteries, begins: "Sentient beings are intrinsically Buddha," and ends, "This very place is the Lotus Land, this very body is Buddha." For Hakuin, then, satori is an experience in which one gains an "awareness of True Self" and in kensho "our own Original Self-Nature presents itself in direct immediacy."[3] But for Hakuin this awareness comes suddenly after a period of time in which one seems quite removed from such realization, if not moving in an opposite direction. In regard to his own case he says that "it was at the age of twenty-four that I first directly experienced the Supremely Important Matter of this Self-Awareness of Original Nature."[4]

Rinzai as well as Soto emphasizes transcending the distinctions between sacred and profane, mind and body, significant and trivial. In short, they both cultivate non-dualistic perspectives. Lin-chi, founder of the Rinzai sect, admonished his monks in words quite similar to Dogen's. "The Way of Buddhism admits of no artificial effort. It only consists of doing the ordinary things without any fuss: going to the stool, making water, putting on clothes, taking a meal, sleeping when tired. Let the fools laugh at me. Only the wise know what I mean. . . ."[5]

Rinzai and Soto share in what, in the Socratic/Platonic tradition, is called the Doctrine of Recollection. Both believe that the Truth is "within." It is immediately accessible to each individual. It is not hopelessly lost or distorted, needing the saving grace of Amida to help restore it. The religious path is, therefore, essentially a matter of remembrance. The highest knowledge is not a distant, inaccessible understanding, but an ever-present reality. The task is to recall what one already knows, to be what one already is. One awakens to what one already understands, but has forgotten, while it is the dim awareness of that intrinsic reality that haunts one and goads one into trying to recollect it. In these terms, the differences between Rinzai and Soto are differences in effecting this remembrance. They are two types of recollection.

Methodological Contrasts

The issue between Rinzai and Soto, then, seems to be primarily a difference in method and psychology rather than philosophy and Buddhology. The Rinzai method and associated psychology is that of bursting the bonds of ego, desire, attachment, and ignorance—to cite some of the root causes of suffering and evil in Buddhist teaching. In Christmas Humphrey's helpful analogy, the Rinzai approach, "like the explosives used in logging, is designed to break the jam in the river, and let the waters and all which float thereon ride free."[6] The Soto approach, on the other hand, to use Alan Watts' imagery, is that "muddy water is best cleared by leaving it alone."[7] To dynamite the pond would only make the pond muddier!

As a corollary of this, a basic difference between the two schools is the respective emphasis of each upon faith and doubt. Faith (*daishinkon*, "great root-faith") is an essential of Zen practice, whether the focus is on koan-zen or zazen, for an important motivating force in one's continuing practice is the firm conviction that this process is the Way of the Buddha, and that it will lead to fuller and deeper insight. Without that faith one will not practice diligently or proceed very far down the Buddhist path. This faith, however, is strongly accented in Soto. Again and again Dogen preached to his monks that they should sit firmly and unwaveringly in the faith that their true nature is Buddha-nature and that their zazen and daily life is the Way of the Buddha. Though this faith is present in Rinzai, it is more in the background, for the immediate foreground of Rinzai is doubt. One must cultivate doubt, great doubt (*daigi*), until every string which ties one to false and illusory ways of thinking and being is cut. One arrives at Buddhist understanding by way of a profound doubt which breaks up and dissolves all those impediments that stand in the way of, and in contradiction to, the realization of one's true nature. The predominant motivating force, the spring that drives the engine of Zen practice, is the tension created by doubt. Rinzai Zen is, naturally, koan-zen, for a relentless meditation upon a koan winds the spring (Hakuin's "doubt mass") tighter and tighter, until some releasing mechanism (a shout, a word, a chance event) lets the spring suddenly uncoil with great force and one has an abrupt sense of insight and freedom.

Koan-zen, then, proceeds on the basis of inner *tension,* whereas the zazen-only approach of Soto proceeds on the basis of inner *harmony.* The koan is a condensation of the fundamental tensions of the divided self or the sick-souled (to use James' terminology); or in Buddhist terms the tensions of the desiring self, tossed back and forth between all the dualities of maya. The contradictory character of the koan focuses these tensions, like a magnifying glass pinpointing the rays of the sun on a piece of paper and burning through it. The immediate aim is not to relax the tensions but to intensify them, driving them deep into the pit of the stomach where they become Hakuin's ''great ball of doubt'' or Mumon's ''red-hot ball of iron.'' Day and night, in daily work as well as in the meditation hall or temple, the concentration is to continue. This concentration is brought to a climax in the periodic weeks of *sesshin* where long periods of koan-meditation, accompanied by the strikings and shoutings of the monitors, a reduction of sleep, and progress checks with the roshi (*sanzen*), combine to produce a maximum of tension. Not surprisingly, many experiences of satori/kensho occur during a *sesshin* (''mind unifying''). As Philip Kapleau comments from his own experiences, ''This strategy of placing the student in a desperate situation where he is relentlessly driven from the rear [by a senior monk or meditation monitor] and vigorously repulsed in front [by the roshi in rejecting his answers and behavior] often builds up pressures within him that lead to that inner explosion without which true satori seldom occurs.''[8]

Kapleau gives several testimonials by American Zen students which illustrate these experiences. ''Perhaps the powerful emotional impact of this experience. . . . was due to the very hopelessness of my condition before it happened: almost completely without faith, dry as a bone, sterile, dull, dead, locked into the vice of skepticism, unable to break free. And yearning always—the hungriest of hungry ghosts.''[9] Another respondent says, ''It is difficult for me even now to believe the point of tension this body-mind had reached before the October session. For six months before I could scarcely eat anything—I lost more than twenty pounds. I was miserable, and for no apparent reason.''[10] A third respondent writes, ''The pressure inside is building, building. The valve opens. . . steam rises and issues forth in a world-shaking blast. . . . The blast is coming out of me, is me, is everyone, everything! Barriers begin to fall; the mind is working feverishly; mysterious sayings become clear. Of course, of course! How wonderful, how right!''[11] A fourth respondent remarks, ''How true that verse about its taking a cold winter to enjoy the plum blossoms in the spring. One feels exactly as though one has just been let out of prison—first Mu takes you and shows you how utterly imprisoned you are, and then it sets you free!''[12] One final example: ''My awakening is as real as getting up in the morning from a meaningless dream and splashing cold water on my face. You laugh to recall the antics you had just been going through in your dream, then take a deep, wonderful breath and go about your business. . . . As I walked down the street yesterday the whole universe was suddenly born.''[13] The Rinzai scenario is unmistakable: *before,* there is pressure, hopelessness, skepticism, misery, bondage; *after* there is rebirth, liberation, release, ecstasy.

A student once questioned Yasutani-roshi during *dokusan* at a *sesshin* about the way the *monjutor* (a meditation assistant, named for Monju, the Buddha of Wisdom) was shouting so loudly and striking everyone so hard during meditation periods. The roshi responded: ''These people are close to kensho, that is why they are being struck so hard—to spur them on to a last desperate effort.''[14] Or when the same student questioned the importance of struggling with the issue of ''I,'' the roshi answered: ''You must come up against this question with the force of a bomb, and all your intellectual notions and ideas must be annihilated. The only way to resolve this question is to come to the explosive inner realization that everything is Nothing.''[15]

In Soto, on the other hand, the approach is quite different. In ''just sitting'' in the faith that one is intrinsically enlightened, pure, whole, and free, and that one's practice proceeds from that ultimate source, one sits in and out of the unity and harmony of the Buddha-nature, like a duck bobbing naturally in water rather than a drowning cat frantically trying to swim. To switch the analogy, the object of one's meditation is not to bring inner and outer tensions to a fever pitch beyond which, when the fever breaks, one may have a sense of release and freedom, but to draw upon the dynamic of one's indestructable health and psycho-physical harmony. If there is a power that comes from tension, there is an even greater power that comes from unity and tranquillity, like the totally relaxed yet fully alert state of the master Zen archer or swordsman, moving gracefully, singlemindedly, seemingly effortlessly. His muscles are not tense but in full readiness. His mind is not taut but alert. He does not receive power from the presence of any enemy or fear of death or a sense of desperation. His actions proceed from a harmonious center which enables him, in turn, to flow harmoniously with the action outside himself.

Thus while Rinzai increases tension by its techniques, Soto decreases tension. It calls for faith that the tensions themselves, whatever they may be, are the world of maya. Rinzai uses the *negative* method of trying to break up illusion and ignorance; Soto uses the *positive* method of building upon one's pre-existent dharma-knowledge and natural serenity. In Rinzai the negative method is justified by the dramatic sense of liberation and explosive insight that may come from the torment. Soto prefers small, everyday insights. If some earth-shaking flash of light comes now and then, fine; but large or small, thundering or quiet as a mouse, is not the issue. What is most important is steady everyday practice on an even keel. In Soto, as it is said, "Everyday is a good day."

Imagery

To some extent the differences between Rinzai and Soto are the result of their respective choices of imagery, which seem more appropriate to one type of experience than to another. The twice-born experiences of Rinzai, and the turmoil and conflict preceding them, suggest the *soteriological* imagery of a *fall* into a state of affairs from which each must be rescued or helped to discover the means of escape. One is variously referred to as being caught, trapped, imprisoned, lost, hopeless, etc. The once-born experiences of Soto, however, suggest the *developmental* imagery of a *rise* toward a spiritual flowering through the proper and normal process of growth—just as the plant, the roots of which are certainly to be found in the darkness and dirt beneath, yet grows out of that condition toward the light and purity of the air above, beckoned by its true destiny, which is also its ultimate origin. The seed of an oak is nothing other than an oak.

If these differences are couched in traditional Mahayana terms,

Rinzai Zen emphasizes "acquired enlightenment" (*shikaku*). One is caught within the maya of an unenlightened consciousness and seeks by means of koan-introspection to break free of this deluded state through a succession of satoris. Nevertheless, acquired enlightenment is not a wholly new acquisition, but as in Soto Zen it is a reclaiming of what one already is and knows. Soto Zen emphasizes this "original enlightenment" (*hongaku*). If such is in fact the center of one's being and knowing, which no one has completely forgotten and from which no one is completely estranged—otherwise it would never occur to anyone to seek enlightenment—then one should sit at and live out of that center. One should make explicit what is already implicit, for one cannot acquire enlightenment, only realize it more fully.

Two traditional sayings in Japanese Zen are especially instructive. The first: "The teaching of Rinzai Zen is like the frost of the late autumn, making one shiver, while the teaching of Soto Zen is like the spring breeze which caresses the flower, helping it to bloom." The second: "Rinzai teaching is like a brave general who moves a regiment without delay, while Soto teaching is like a farmer taking care of a rice field, one stalk after another, patiently."[16] The first saying underlines the Rinzai emphasis upon killing the old self (late autumn) as a prelude to the rebirth of the new self, whereas Soto goes directly to the spring images of seed, growth, and coming to flower. The second saying underlines the dramatic, heroic, even militaristic emphasis of Rinzai, set to do battle with ego, desire and illusion. The image of the brave general is contrasted to the quietistic, nurturing emphasis of Soto—the rice farmer cultivating the field of the Buddha Dharma. Clearly both sayings correspond in imagery and psychology with the twice-born and once-born perspectives respectively, as well as the contrasting characteristics of what in ancient China were known as the *yang* (masculine, aggressive) and *yin* (feminine, passive) approaches.

Addressing Different Conditions

The implication of all this would seem to be that, originally, these two approaches have arisen out of and addressed themselves to two different human conditions. Subsequently they have tended to become, if not strictly orthodoxies, then at least matters of orthopraxy. There are, however, masters in both the Rinzai and Soto schools who have used the techniques of both traditions, and there are even some who have adopted the practice from Pure Land of chanting the *nembutsu*. The more flexible approach is, at least, more in accord with the traditional Indian (both Hindu and Buddhist) understanding of the role of the guru as a spiritual physician who adapts his medicine and therapy to the specific condition of the disciple, rather than giving the same prescription to all regardless of differing constitutions and maladies. There is, of course, a term for this in traditional Buddhism—*upaya* (accommodating method)—which is used to explain and justify the many sects of Buddhism and their great variety of practices. The Buddhas, Bodhisattvas, Patriarchs, and teachers are all said to use *upaya,* adjusting their teaching and methods to the specific character, situation, and level of understanding of those being taught. Because of the considerable variety of individual circumstances, there cannot be one right way of teaching and practising Buddhism, though the fundamental principles and ideals of Buddhism remain constant.

Whatever the technique, both Zen schools recognize that at a certain point (either from the beginning in "just sitting" or through some dramatic change in the psyche) the goal must become a non-goal, seeking must turn into no-seeking, action into non-action. As Bodhidharma is reputed to have said, "All the attainments of the Buddhas are really non-attainments."[17] Or as the sixth Ch'an patriarch Hui-neng preached: "When there is no abiding of thought anywhere on anything—this is being unbound. This not abiding anywhere is the root of our life."[18] On this point both Hakuin and Dogen agree. However the moment is arrived at, one's Buddha nature is realized at the moment when the desiring self is no longer a self desiring, even a self desiring to become a Buddha.

Not only does Dogen advise, "Do not think about how to become a Buddha," but Lin-chi (Rinzai) before him had also characterized the true Zen individual as one who has "not a thought of running after Buddhahood. He is free from such pinings."[19] In words remarkably similar to Dogen's, Lin-chi had also maintained that the true seeker does not seek. He simply "walks when he wants to walk, and sits when he wants to sit, without a single thought of seeking Buddhahood. . . . Do not follow others who are busying themselves aimlessly with their studies of Ch'an and Tao, their learning of names and sayings, and their quest of Buddha, Patriarchs and enlightened masters. . . . If your searching minds really come to an end, there will be no more anxiety for anything."[20]

The obvious problem, then, and the basis of the difference between Rinzai and Soto—in Lin-chi's own words—is how searching minds are really to come to an end where there will be no more anxiety for anything. For Dogen this state is the original, fundamental, and therefore perfectly natural and central state of one's being in which one should just sit. For Hakuin the state of ego, desire, attachment, and ignorance into which one has fallen must be broken out of in order that one might return to living out of the purity of one's original self-nature. One realizes moments of doing so in successive experiences of satori and their after-effects, and thereby is increasingly able to do so.

Judging from Hakuin's own testimony, Dogen's "just sitting" would not have worked for him. He was too inwardly divided and too beset by melancholy, guilt, and doubt. "Just sitting" for Hakuin became "dead sitting" and, if anything, aroused the opposite of its intention: he became increasingly agitated, anxious, distracted, and depressed. One almost hears an echo of the cry of the Apostle Paul: "O wretched man that I am, who shall deliver me from this body of death?" (Romans 7:24). Hakuin needed something that would bring his internal conflicts out into the open and to a climax. And for this the *koan* served admirably as a device for "snapping the bonds of ignorance."

One might ask, however, whether all who enter a Rinzai monastery are to be seen as similarly troubled souls in need of such dramatic techniques to effect a break in the chains of ignorance and bring release from the dungeon into the light, or whether instead such techniques are sometimes being used to create in relatively stable spirits a sense of doubt, anxiety, and despair, from which they can have in turn a sense of release. According to Rinzai teaching, tensions, whether generated by internal or external causes, are extremely helpful in producing the determination to win through to a satori experience; and someone whose life is relatively free from tensions is seen as likely to come to a breaking point more slowly than someone who is deeply troubled or whose self-confidence is shaky. The same techniques that are used to bring pre-existent tensions and doubts to a climax—koans, verbal abuse, shouting, striking—are therefore also used to produce tensions and doubts in those who were free from them. Relatively untroubled souls are systematically troubled in order to bring them to the exhilarating experience of becoming untroubled again. This is analogous to a lifeguard who, having no actual cases of drowning swimmers to ply his skills upon, throws people into the water and dunks them repeatedly until they begin to gasp for breath and take on water, in order to give them the experience of drowning and the joy of being saved from drowning!

From a Soto standpoint, there is also the danger that any emphasis upon what Abraham Maslow has called "peak experiences" will lead to an emphasis upon the ecstatic character of the experience itself, rather than upon the insight that experience provided. The concern then becomes one of having an emotional high, and repeating that "peak" as often as possible. There is the further danger that such mountain-top experiences will be so dramatic and pleasurable that the world of ordinary experiences and commonplace events will be deprecated—including the more ordinary and commonplace experiences in the relatively unexciting lives of the once-born. The distinctions between sacred and profane, marvelous and everyday, may be intensified rather than collapsed.

Five Types of Zen

Yasutani-roshi has distinguished between five types of Zen—using the word in its broadest possible sense. 1) The most elementary type is *bompu* (ordinary) Zen, which simply is concerned with developing the powers of concentration (*joriki*) and with the improvements that can be brought thereby to one's general physical and mental well-being and to the quality of one's efforts in this or that arena. This would correspond to the general level of interest in yoga in the West as merely an efficacious form of physical and mental exercise. 2) The second type is *gedo* (outside way) Zen, which is any form of meditational practice outside the Buddhist tradition; some of the presuppositions, techniques and aims may be similar to those in Buddhist meditation, but some are also different. 3) The third type is *shojo* (Small Vehicle or Hinayana Buddhism). This is that form of Buddhist meditation which seeks individual release from the world of samsara, birth and rebirth. It aims to achieve the state of *mushinjo* (a trance-like state of no-thought), but which does not go on beyond seeking individual release to that full enlightenment which sees all existence as an interdependent and inseparable whole. 4) The fourth type of Zen is *daijo* (Great Vehicle or Mahayana Buddhism), the aim of which is satori and kensho—both obviously defined by Yasutani in Rinzai terms. 5) The fifth type of Zen is *saijojo* (Highest Vehicle), which is said to be the practice of enlightened Buddhas; it is therefore not a form of practice seeking enlightenment, but rather the pure expression of enlightenment.[21]

In terms of this classification, the issue lies largely between the last two forms. Surprisingly, Yasutani identifies the fifth and highest form of meditation with the Soto school. *Daijo* Zen is the koan-introspection of Rinzai, whereas *saijojo* Zen is the zazen-only of Soto. He even defines the *saijojo* type in terms characteristic of Dogen, i.e., that it is not a means to an end but rather the end itself. It is the meditation of non-seeking. Yasutani then comments that "the Rinzai sect places *daijo* uppermost and *saijojo* beneath, whereas the Soto sect does the reverse. In *saijojo*, when rightly practiced, you sit in the firm conviction that zazen is the actualization of your undefiled True-nature."[22]

Yasutani argues that the two approaches are complementary, with Rinzai emphasizing means and Soto the end—though he should add that in Soto the end is the beginning. In any case, they are not to be seen as mutually exclusive positions, for Rinzai too stresses that zazen is not only a means but an end (the practice of Buddhas), and that what one is seeking for (enlightenment, Buddha-nature) is what one really is. Soto, on the other hand, while stressing intrinsic enlightenment and one's original nature as Buddha, also acknowledges a difference between those who fully realize this and live out of that realization and those who do not.

Yasutani attempted to draw upon both traditions and to give them equal, complementary value. In certain contexts, however, Rinzai practice was given the higher value. On the one hand *saijojo* is said to be "the highest vehicle, the culmination and crown of Buddhist Zen, practiced by all the Buddhas of the past—viz., Shakyamuni and Amida—and. . . the expression of absolute life, life in its purest form. . . [involving] no struggle for satori or any other object. . .[for] in this highest practice means and ends coalesce."[23] Nevertheless, when

81

Yasutani describes the four levels of aspiration, meditation on the koan is placed at the top as most suitable for those with highest aspiration, "determined to realize their true self. . . secure in the knowledge that by doing so they can realize their goal in the shortest time."[24] In this scheme the *shikantaza* of the Soto school is placed third, below koan-zen and above only those with mere curiosity and those interested only in physical and mental health (*bompu* zen). Those who practice Dogen's *shikantaza* alone are said to be those who "want to tread the path of the Buddha [and] have established faith in the reality of the enlightenment experience. . . though the resolve to attain it has not yet been awakened."[25] This is a travesty of Dogen's position and experience. Although Yasutani had previously acknowledged that zazen in Soto is not a means to an end but is an end in itself, here he speaks of Soto meditation in Rinzai terms as a means to an end.

Though Yasutani has claimed to present the two traditions as equal and complementary perspectives, he places the koan-method above the *shikantaza* of Soto (which is *not* a method of attaining enlightenment, as he previously notes), and thus misconstrues the meaning of zazen-only for Dogen. Zazen (or *shikantaza*) proceeds from one's intrinsic enlightenment, as does one's faith in one's intrinsic enlightenment. Faith is continuously being confirmed by understanding. It is not that one struggles for months or years in darkness and doubt to the point of desperation and despair, and in the hope of a breakthrough at the end of the tunnel. One sits and moves about in the confidence that the ox on which one is riding through the country-side is the ox for which one had set out in search. Dogen says to his monks, "Understand that although you train in the world of delusion, enlightenment is already there."[26]

It should be acknowledged, however, that if Rinzai meditation has its pitfalls, so does Soto. Rinzai tends to turn Zen practice into a means to an end, to be interminably goal-oriented. And the end that is emphasized (*satori*) may be the ecstasy involved in the experience rather than the insight (*kensho*) which issues from the experience. Soto, on the other hand, may play only in the shallow waters of mental control (*joriki*) instead of moving more deeply and fully into a realization and expression of one's Buddha nature. Instead of living more and more out of the immediacy of original enlightenment and allowing that to pervade more and more of one's life, one may be satisfied to merely enjoy the momentary therapeutic benefits of "sitting quietly, doing nothing," and to use faith in one's original nature to rationalize the status quo. Rather than being the highest level of Zen practice (*saijojo*), the practice of Buddhas, Soto is in danger of reducing itself to the lowest level, *bompu* zen. If Rinzai can become artificial in its method, Soto can become superficial in its realization.

CHAPTER VI

Something Wonderful, Nothing Special

The foregoing interpretation of the two schools of Zen is in general accord with William James' efforts at presenting a balanced and sympathetic analysis of both once-born and twice-born types of religious experience. "Why in the name of common sense need we assume that only one such system of ideas can be true? The obvious outcome of our total experience is that the world can be handled according to many systems of ideas, and is so handled by different men, and will each time give some characteristic kind of profit. . . while at the same time some other kind of profit has to be omitted or postponed."[1]

A Twice-Born Bias

Despite James' evenhandedness, however, he nevertheless came to the conclusion (which one also finds in Yasutani and among Rinzai advocates generally) that the once-born perspective omits more from its purview than does the twice-born, and that the twice-born perspective has more depth, richness, profundity and completeness than the once-born. "There is no doubt that healthy-mindedness is inadequate as a philosophical doctrine, because the evil facts which it refuses positively to account for are a genuine portion of reality; and they may after all be the best key to life's significance, and possibly the only openers of our eyes to the deepest levels of truth."[2]

A part of James' motivation for his study of religious experience appears to have been his special fascination with extraordinary states of consciousness. In his introduction to the *Varieties* he remarks that "our normal waking consciousness is but one special type of consciousness, whilst all admit that, parted from it by the flimsiest of screens, there lie potential forms of consciousness entirely different." After surveying the heights and depths of these unusual states, he concludes that "systematic healthy-mindedness is formally less complete than systems that give prominence to dark and abysmal realities. The completest religions would therefore seem to be those in which pessimistic elements are best developed."[4] Both Christianity and Buddhism are cited as the clearest examples of these "religions of deliverance" from conditions otherwise very pessimistically described.

The suggestion that once-born experience is intrinsically superficial, unavoidably inadequate, or even willfully ignorant concerning evil and suffering is an unfortunate one for James' analysis, and is arrived at by questionable means. At the least, it is a curious conclusion to see greater wisdom in the extremism and imbalances of tortured spirits and to award the reputation of greater profundity to sickness of soul, while attributing a foolhardy optimism to relatively stable spirits and taking normal, healthy patterns of growth as evidence of shallowness. One might well argue that the person who develops more normally, without falling victim to the great conflicts and traumas of the sick-souled, is in possession of the very wisdom and grace and equanimity for which the sick-souled so desperately seek. A second birth may be a great blessing for those in the depths of psychic turmoil, but it is hardly therefore the paradigmatic ideal for all. And the attempt to provoke such an experience in others by artificially inducing crises, conflicts, and doubts may be a thoroughly irresponsible form of cruelty. It is as if one were to be made to feel sinful and guilty for not having felt sinful and guilty, in order that one might experience release from sin and guilt and no longer feel sinful and guilty! As Alan Watts has suggested, this can be like walking about in lead boots until totally exhausted in order to have the exhilarating experience of taking them off again.[5]

If one tests James' conclusions by the Japanese cases here studied and compares Hakuin and Dogen, Dogen is certainly not lacking in any sort of depth, richness, profundity, or completeness. Indeed, Dogen has been judged by many Japanese and Western scholars to be one of the greatest philosophers and religious teachers in Japanese history. Nor is Dogen guilty of an easy optimism or given to ignoring evil and suffering. Dogen is as much a realist as Hakuin, and the issue is not one of ignoring the problems of evil and suffering, but the best way of understanding and dealing with them.

James may have been led to greater sympathy with the twice-born perspective in part because he himself was of the twice-born type. In his diary he reveals that, as a youth, he had been subject to melancholy and morbidity. In this he was like his father, and very unlike his "healthy-minded" mother. He even indicates that at one point in his life "suicide seemed the most manly form to put my daring to." It is generally acknowledged that James in his *Varieties* includes his own case under the guise of a Frenchman whose confession he pretends to "translate freely," with "permission to print" thankfully received from "the sufferer."

> Whilst in this state of philosophic pessimism and general depression of spirits about my prospects, I went one evening into a dressing room in the twilight to procure some article that was there; when suddenly there fell upon me without any warning, just as if it came out of the darkness, a horrible fear of my own existence. Simultaneously there arose in my mind the image of an epileptic patient whom I had seen in the asylum. . . . This image and my fear entered into a species of combination with each other. *That shape am I,* I felt, potentially. . . . I became a mass of quivering fear. After this the universe was changed for me altogether. I awoke morning after morning with a horrible dread at the pit of my stomach, and with a sense of the insecurity of life that I never knew before, and that I have never felt since. It was like a revelation; and although the immediate feelings passed away, the experience has made me sympathetic with the morbid feelings of others ever since.[6]

This is the last case James gives under the caption of the "sick soul," and he refers to it as "the worst kind of melancholy. . . which takes the form of panic fear." He concludes his account with a reference to his (the "Frenchman's") healthy-minded mother.

> In general I dreaded to be left alone. I remember
> wondering how other people could live, how I
> myself had ever lived, so unconscious of that pit
> of insecurity beneath the surface of life. My mother
> in particular, a very cheerful person, seemed to
> me a perfect paradox in her unconsciousness of
> danger, which you may well believe I was very
> careful not to disturb by revelations of my own state
> of mind. I have always thought that this experience
> of melancholia of mine had a religious bearing.[7]

These quotations not only indicate James' twice-born bent, but also both his difficulties in understanding the healthy-minded, who seem so cheerfully oblivious to the dangers and insecurities lurking beneath the "surface of life," and his sympathies "with the morbid feelings of others." After citing his own case, incognito, James then concludes that the healthy-minded betray a kind of childlike innocence and lack of maturity in comparison with those things which the sick-souled see and experience. Of the three types of cases he considers under the latter category, he remarks: "one of them gives us the vanity of mortal things; another the sense of sin; and the remaining one describes the fear of the universe; and in one or other of these three ways it always is that man's original optimism and self-satisfaction get leveled with the dust."[8]

Problems also arise in James' analysis because he too closely associates the once-born typology, if not with his "perfect paradox" of a mother, with the teachings of certain liberal religious movements of late 19th-century America, especially the Ethical Culture, Mind-Cure, and Christian Science societies. The teachings of these particular groups are certainly not logically necessary consequences of the type of personality and experience that he has begun to analyze. He also cites the poet Walt Whitman and certain Unitarians, such as Edward Hale and Theodore Parker, as his initial examples; yet the teachings of these various groups and individuals are hardly the same. The implied movement from a certain psychological type to a certain philosophical and religious position is not without some significant leaps.

Edward Hale's own account of his religious experience and

outlook indicates quite clearly from the start what the issues are for the once-born type:

> I observe, with profound regret, the religious strug-
> gles which come into many biographies, as if
> almost essential to the formation of the hero. . . .
> Any man has an advantage, not to be estimated,
> who is born, as I was, into a family where the
> religion is simple and rational; who is trained in
> the theory of such a religion, so that he never
> knows, for an hour, what these religious or
> irreligious struggles are. . . . To live with all my
> might seemed to me easy; to learn where there was
> so much to learn seemed pleasant and almost of
> course; to lend a hand, if one had a chance,
> natural.[9]

The issues for Hale are not at all what James finally makes of them: optimism versus pessimism (do not the twice-born eventually become rather optimistic and even quite manic at times?); self-satisfaction versus self-doubt, insecurity, anxiety and guilt; and a profound versus a shallow view of evil and suffering. Rather, the issues center on the differences between a *cataclysmic* view of psychic development and an *organic* view. The organic view sees develop-ment into wholeness and maturity as a natural process of growth, while the cataclysmic view can only find wholeness and maturity at the end of a dark tunnel or bewildering labyrinth, and after a tortuous process of inner and outer struggle.

James confuses the issues by crediting the once-born type with an inordinate optimism which "deliberately excludes evil from its field of vision,"[10] and a sentimental romanticism "whose affinities are rather with flowers and birds and all enchanting innocencies than with dark human passions."[11] Francis Newman, from whom James had adopted his typology, had similarly viewed the once-born as naive and simplistic, with a kind of child's innocence in their lack of a deep sense of evil in themselves or in the world. Yet in the case just cited from James, Dr. Hale does not exclude evil or ignore dark human passions. He "observes, with profound regret," these tragic conflicts that wreak havoc in the lives of others and those about them. What he refuses to do is to see the sick and divided self as "essential to the formation of the hero." He insists on the naturalness and normalcy of his own spiritual evolution in which enthusiasm came easily, faith simply, altruism naturally, and learning pleasantly. And instead of idealizing the heroic dramas of the twice-born and holding them up as religious models to be emulated, he sees his own type of situation as most fortunate and, ideally, normative.

James had also cited similar sentiments from another noted Unitarian, Theodore Parker, who wrote: "I have done wrong things enough in my life, and do them now; I miss the mark, draw bow, and try again. But I am not conscious of hating God, or man, or right, or love, and I know there is much 'health in me'; and in my body, even now, there dwelleth many a good thing, spite of consumption and Saint Paul."[12] If James had stayed with the affirmations and concerns of these initial examples—along with Walt Whitman whom he also cites—and drawn out their implications, he might have developed a typology of once-born experience that was as accurate and useful as his characterizations of the twice-born. Instead he went on to cite examples from Ethical Culture, Mind-Cure, and Christian Science as if the peculiarities of their positions were the direct intellectual consequence of once-born experience, and its inevitable conclusion.

Both the initial examples he cites (Hale, Parker, Whitman) and the Japanese example of Dogen that I have cited, suggest that the once-born perspective on self and world is no less profound, mature, rich, and complete than the twice-born. They also suggest that no single religious or philosophical position can be seen as a concomitant of either the once-born or the twice-born type, or as a logical deduction from either. Hakuin's twice-born experiences are interpreted as the sudden breakthrough into one's "Original Self-Nature," whereas the Apostle Paul or Martin Luther or Shinran interpreted their experiences as the sudden inbreaking of an external grace, accepting and saving them from a pervasive sinfulness. Dogen, similarly, interprets his experiences within the frame of reference defined by the Tendai and Zen schools of Buddhism and within an Oriental (rather than Indian) context. Hale and Parker interpret their experiences within the frame of reference of a Unitarian Protestantism in the American context of 19th-century New England.

With these qualifications, James' typology would still seem to have continuing utility, and to be particularly helpful in elucidating the differences between Rinzai and Soto Zen. Having been critical of James' association of an easy and innocent optimism with the once-born, it would not do to leave the suggestion that he is entirely wrong in this. For if the weakness of the twice-born is that they tend to paint the world too darkly, the weakness of the once-born is that they tend to paint the world too lightly. And if the twice-born are inclined to undervalue more ordinary experiences, the once-born are inclined to discount twice-born sensitivities and visions.

The fact is, of course, that both psychology and religion have displayed far more interest, energy, and ingenuity in dealing with the sick-souled or divided self than they have in dealing with the healthy-minded. What is needed both in psychology and religion is a comparable development of a psychology of the once-born, and an interpretation of the religious profundity and maturity of such a perspective on life. In the Zen context, Dogen provides a very helpful starting point for this, both psychologically and religiously.

Zen "Peakers" and "Non-Peakers"

In more recent psychological theory, Abraham Maslow has also dealt with the twice-born type under the more generalized category of "peak experiences." An application of his typology to the Zen examples cited may prove helpful. Though his treatment is not completely parallel to James' typology, he does attribute considerable importance to the role of peak experiences in psychological development. He distinguishes between "peakers," who have had the many benefits Maslow associates with peak experiences, and "non-peakers" who have very few such experiences. The experiences the "non-peakers" have is at best low key, and they share in the benefits primarily in a vicarious manner by identifying with certain "peakers."

"Peakers" provide leadership on the basis of the visions provided by their peak experiences, and by various qualities that result from them. Such people become what Maslow calls "self-actualized" individuals, examples (and therefore exemplars) of the most creative, visionary, mature, self-motivated, fully-developed, highly evolved human beings—to use some of Maslow's designations.[13] Presumably we are to believe that Hakuin, who certainly had his share of peak experiences, is to be awarded the title and attributes of the "self-actualized individual," while Dogen as a non-peaker is not.

The nature of those peak experiences which bestow such

91

beatitudes is characterized by Maslow as 1) tending to come suddenly, with a sense of surprise; 2) bringing an experience of unity and wholeness; 3) having the flavor of awe, wonder, reverence, humility, surrender; 4) involving a loss of the sense of time and space; 5) marked by passivity and receptivity relative to something happening to oneself or within oneself; and 6) culminating in a feeling of pure gratification, elation, and joy. Such experiences seem self-validating and self-justifying, and tend to become absolute points of reference, with other events seen relative to them or as relativized by them. "Numerous writers on aesthetics, religion, creativeness and love uniformly describe these experiences not only as valuable intrinsically, but also as *so* valuable that they make life worthwhile by their occasional occurrence. The mystics have always affirmed the supreme value of the great mystic experience, which may come only two or three times in a lifetime."[14]

The after-effects of such an experience are described as therapeutic—relative to prior neurosis—freeing the individual from blockages, inhibitions, fears, doubts, etc., altering the person's view of himself and the world, releasing greater creativity and expressiveness, making life seem worthwhile, and leaving the person with a desire to repeat the peak experience. Maslow summarizes the effects of a peak experience by likening it to "a visit to a personally defined Heaven from which the person then returns to earth."[15] As a result, attempts at communicating during or following a peak experience "tend often to become poetic, mythical and rhapsodic, as if this were the natural kind of language to express such states of being."[16]

A peak experience, therefore, tends to become an end-in-itself. And since it is supremely worth having, everything else is revalued (and usually devalued) according to it, and as of comparatively lesser worth may legitimately be set aside in favor of it, or sacrificed in hope of its repetition. "The peak experiences of pure delight are for my subjects among the ultimate goals of living and the ultimate validations and justifications for it."[17]

Actually, Rinzai Zen recognizes the dangers as well as the desirability of such peak experiences. Those who savor their experience of satori are said to "reek" or "stink" of Zen, either because of their sense of pride in their achievement—in direct contradiction to the realization of the folly of ego and desire that is supposedly a part of the kensho in the experience—or because of an emphasis on the ecstasy rather than the insight (kensho) involved. Thus Harada-roshi chides a lay disciple with "smelling the awful smell of enlightenment" and notes that "even the honored Shakyamuni clung to the taste of his enlightenment for a period of three weeks." He then added: "My own sickness lasted about ten years. Ha!"[18]

Maslow's description of peak experience, like James' twice-born typology, certainly fits the religious experience and self-understanding of Hakuin. But it provides very little basis for understanding Dogen, and a good deal of basis for *mis*understanding Dogen and the type of religious experience and self-understanding he represents. If a non-peaker is the rough equivalent of James' once-born, Maslow's analysis provides even less basis than that of James for appreciating the forms of self-actualization, creativity, maturity, and leadership available to those who do not have peak experiences and do not place high value upon them. And his analysis perpetuates the deprecation of ordinary, commonplace, everyday sorts of states and experiences on the grounds that they are less colorful, less interesting, and presumably less profound.

Soto master Shunryu Suzuki offers the following counter-advice to his students: "Zen is not some kind of excitement, but concentration on our usual everyday routine. . . . If possible, try to be always calm and joyful and keep yourself from excitement. . . . Zen is not something to get excited about. . . Do not be too interested in Zen. . . Our unexciting way of practice may appear to be very negative. This is not so. It is a wise and effective way to work on ourselves. It is just very plain."[19]

It was stated earlier that Rinzai Zen seems to foster sudden enlightenment and Soto to foster a gradual approach. Addressing the issue of gradual versus sudden enlightenment, Suzuki remarks: "It may seem as if I am speaking about gradual attainment. This is not so either. In fact, this [i.e., Soto] is the sudden way, because when your practice is calm and ordinary, everyday life itself is enlightenment."[20] Suzuki goes on to say about zazen, "If you continue this simple practice every day, you will obtain some wonderful power. Before you attain it, it is something wonderful, but after you attain it, it is nothing special. . . . So try not to seek something in particular;

93

try not to achieve anything special. You already have everything in your own pure quality. If you understand this ultimate fact, there is no fear."[21]

Neither William James nor Abraham Maslow were capable of dealing fairly and fully with this type of perspective and understanding. Maslow is even less capable than James. If on the one extreme we have a theory of value such as John Dewey's instrumentalism in which everything becomes a means to some other end and nothing is truly an end in itself, in Maslow we have a theory in which certain rare peak experiences are such supremely valuable and insightful ends in themselves that everything else may be turned into means toward these ends. The problem in both cases is the same: in what way can *everything* be seen as a legitimate end in itself, however simple, lowly, menial, insignificant, commonplace, ordinary, profane? How can "everyday life itself [be] enlightenment?" Where is the wisdom in that which is "just very plain?" What is so special in that which is "nothing special"?

Dogen and Soto Zen have an answer to these questions. Perhaps if James and Maslow had known of this other Buddhist tradition and studied it, the once-born and the non-peakers would have received a more appreciative interpretation. Somewhat ironically, the appreciation for the commonplace is one to which Maslow himself came toward the end of his life. After his busy and productive professional career was suddenly halted by a near-fatal heart attack, he commented that "one very important aspect of the post-mortem life is that everything gets precious, gets piercingly important. You get stabbed by things, by flowers and by babies and by beautiful things—just the very act of living, of walking and breathing and eating and having friends and chatting. Everything seems to look more beautiful rather than less, and one gets the much-intensified sense of miracles."[22]

Perhaps it would not be inappropriate, though a bit irreverent, to suggest that a heart attack qualifies as a peak experience. If so, it is certainly not a peak experience that dulls all other experiences by comparison, or that seeks to recapture itself in prayers for repeated peaks! It is not likely to become an end-in-itself. A heart attack can be only one thing: a jolt, a bit of internal shock therapy, awakening one to no new heights or sublime ecstasies but to what has always been there, readily available, profoundly simple, perfectly ordinary, but unnoticed or only half-noticed in the usual distracted awareness of the present moment: When one stops staring at the moon it becomes possible for even fireflies to illumine the night.

EPILOGUE

Two Contemporary Zen Cases

The two contrasting cases of Zen experience that have been the focus of this study—Dogen's and Hakuin's—are both Japanese and come from a far different time from our own. It might be asked whether their experiences and philosophies are such that they could only arise in a Japanese (or more broadly, Oriental) context, or whether they may be found also in modern Western dress.

Consider, then, two contrasting cases of Zen experience, both contemporary, both Western, both involving diligent Zen practice. One practitioner has been attracted to and has successfully pursued a Rinzai form of Zen; the other has taken up practice under a Soto master and found that path especially suitable and helpful.

A Modern Rinzai Case

The first case is offered by the American Rinzai master, Philip Kapleau, as a good example of someone who has achieved a dramatic spiritual breakthrough following a period of considerable inner turmoil and earnest searching. In general outline the symptoms, the mental state, and the flow of events are familiar to the literature of Rinzai. There is also a similarity to the variety of other cases cited by Kapleau in his *Three Pillars of Zen* and *Zen: Dawn in the West*.

In this instance the individual reports that, prior to his first encounter with Zen, his "spiritual life had been one flounder after another until. . . exhausted and depressed, I started sitting [in meditation]." But in his early attempt at Zen practice the initial result was

97

that "it awakened in some way a fear of death, which was to haunt me almost without respite for the next two years. I was saturated by terrible anxiety and psychological numbness. I was terrified of being alone. On one occasion I was so sure that I was going to die that I stopped the car and got out so that I would not die unattended."

Zen practice was continued, however, with the encouragement of the roshi, who counseled—in characteristic Rinzai fashion—that deep anxieties would serve to drive one more deeply into the problem and give greater profundity to one's meditational practice. The more desperate the sense of one's predicament the more energy that could be generated, and the better the chance of bringing internal pressures to a significant breaking point. As if to aid such a process, further symptoms began to surface while the first terrors still continued. "During one hot summer I developed insomnia accompanied by excruciating tensions, and this was to plague me for eighteen months. My teacher urged me to go on with zazen."

Some time later the practitioner attended the *rohatsu sesshin* (a period of intensive meditation in December, commemorating the Buddha's enlightenment). With a feeling that a critical juncture was in the offing, "I flung myself totally into the koan [the *Mu* koan commonly used for novices]. The next few days were lived in unmitigated fury. Urged on by the kyosaku [the striking stick], the shouts of the monjutors [meditation leaders] and the urging of the roshi, I tried to get deeper into my koan, but thoughts always persisted. Try as I might during the work period and mealtimes to stay focused on the koan, my mind wandered. . . The old doubts crept in: I can never do this; those who have passed their first koan are on the staff; they are all young and can take it. . . . It was hopeless, and with that, despair rose up."

Such feelings, however, were countered by a sense that it was his duty to see the matter through, and that to fail to achieve some sort of kensho would be to fail the master and others who had worked so hard to help him through the labyrinth. "An awful responsibility became mine. I could not let the sesshin down. The force of the entire sesshin seemed to become focused in my hara [abdominal region]. The shoulders, arms and stomach were all relaxed but there was this mighty concentrated force at work. The struggle took on titanic proportions. Dry periods came, but my impatience was too much for them. It was just as though one were smashing through a wall.''

Then doubts began to set in again. ''I rushed to dokusan but came back bewildered. Roshi had questioned me, had helped me, but when I came back a doubt about him arose. 'He is going to pass me too easily. He is not deeply enlightened and doesn't want anyone else to be'. The monjutor struck me. It hurt. 'This whole Zen business is a hoax! Harada-roshi admitted that all he did was sell water by the river. There is nothing in it!' I struggled with a sinking feeling of being all alone, utterly forsaken.'' The week-long sesshin, furthermore, was soon coming to a close, and no breakthrough seemed in sight. Everything appeared to be for nought.

After more periods of elation and despair the practitioner experienced a great fear of death, followed by its opposite, the fear of not being able to die. Finally the concern for either possibility vanished, and there remained only the awareness of a vast empty space. In this case the emptiness was not one of feeling alone and forsaken. The sensation was one of ''wholeness and completeness. There was no feeling of needing to control. Perfect but natural liberation.'' He went to the roshi for the last time—the sesshin was officially over—to have this new experience validated, or rejected, as the case might be. The master questioned him three times about the Mu koan. On the third interrogation ''the question suddenly went deep and an eruption, a volcano, roared up from the hara. I shouted 'This is Mu! Mu! Mu!' I was yelling and laughing, 'Lovely Mu! By God, this is Mu!'.''

He then describes the ecstatic feelings that continued for some time afterwards. ''Eight or nine hours after leaving the roshi we arrived home. That night was passed sleeplessly. Limitless, joyful peace. I was exhausted but could not sleep, so great was my joy. Throughout the rest of the week and beyond there has persisted the feeling of being unobstructed, of walking on my own feet, of seeing with my own eyes. . . . A veritable explosion had occurred, but debris remains. Old habits, mind states, reactions—they are still there. But they have lost their grip. Old enemies rise up, crumble and turn to dust, and that tyrant the old dead king is broken, he need be fed no longer.''[1]

A Modern Soto Case

A second, and quite contrasting, case is that of a young man who took up Zen practice at a Soto center in Chicago. His motivations in beginning Zen practice and in pursuing it were quite different. He had read some books on Zen before venturing to come to a meditation hour. The books, however, were based on the Rinzai tradition, with emphasis upon koan usage and satori experience. This led initially to confusion and misunderstanding, as well as false expectations—all of which presented problems at first. Once the situation was clarified a normal process of development began, more suited to his particular temperament.

"I had come to the Zen center mostly out of curiosity. That is, I did not feel some deep compulsion driving me, no profound disquiet or dissatisfaction. I was not aware of any particular anxiety or turmoil. Nor was I moved by any burning existential questions about life and death, meaning or meaninglessness. I have always tended to take life more or less as it comes; and I have always enjoyed investigating new things. My question was a relatively simple one: What is Zen about? What went on in this grey row-house sandwiched inbetween an assortment of other tenement houses on Halsted Street? It seemed somewhat absurdly situated there in the first place, quite out of its Japanese context, with no sand and moss gardens or monastery walls or venerable cedars, only a sign across the front in Japanese and English to distinguish it as the ZEN BUDDHIST TEMPLE OF CHICAGO.

"I had always been inquisitive about things Oriental. As far back as I can remember I had a missionary aunt who was off in that part of the world converting the natives, and periodically sending back cards and pictures and scrolls with strange scenes and markings from another world. There were also the war movies and comic book caricatures of the Japanese which left toothy images of inscrutability, serenity, and deviousness. Now that we were well into our third Asian military involvement in as many decades, this exotic world was getting closer, and the university marketplace was buzzing with talk about the East. Gurus and yogis and swamis seemed to be coming by the boatloads. And along with incense and chanting and Hatha-yoga classes and vegetarian diets came Zen.

"The word itself had an intriguing ring about it. Books were pouring out thick and fast on Zen meditation, Zen koans, Zen anecdotes, Zen poetry. There were books, too, on Zen and Tea, Zen and Archery, Zen and Haiku, Zen and Gardens, Zen and Flower Arrangement, and Zen and Motorcycle Maintenance. It was all part of a fascinating new world which was opening up, offering a sense of mystery and adventure, new perspectives on all aspects of life, and perhaps the promise of treasures not found in Western civilization.

"In the excitement and exploratory zeal of that era I visited the Zen center with some friends. We were not conversions-in-the-making, but we were open to something new, and we came with a mood of expectancy. It *was* another world: straw mats and black cushions, a small altar at one end with a Buddha-image and incense burning, a gong and drum to one side, plain walls save for an ink-sketch of Bodhidharma frowning upon the scene. 'Take off your shoes in the hall and tip-toe in silence, sit on a cushion, and face the wall'. There were some brief instructions on posture and procedure given by two young assistants in black robes and distant faces. When the roshi entered the 'service' began. Standing, facing the altar, we mumbled along to a short Buddhist chant (the Heart Sutra) in Japanese, whereupon all sat cross-legged for a seemingly interminable forty-five minutes of wall-gazing, while the roshi went about adjusting postures or striking a few regulars on the shoulder with his oak stick. We then stood for a repeat of the same chant, paid our respects at the altar, and left.

"Certain that I had missed something the first time, and more curious than ever what all the Zen fuss was about, I returned for further sessions and for private instruction with the roshi. I had read several books on Zen, and it seemed considerably more colorful and exciting than this. Where was Baso's shout or Rinzai's lion-roar? Where were the koan-riddles? Where was the eccentric and unpredictable behavior for which Zen masters were supposed to be notorious? When would we move on to dredging up the dark inner forces of maya, or arrive at those ecstatic experiences that had left such a trail of people from China to Japan shouting and laughing and leaping about?

"The roshi said that I should just sit quietly and stop questioning. The questioning mind was to be turned off. It was like a high-power motorboat dashing noisily about the surface of the lake; one could never see into the depths or catch any fish in that fashion. I was not to think about anything, not even Buddhist things, much less exciting Buddhist things. That just churned up the water more. After a storm the lake just sits, and everything returns to normal. If thought-waves came, I was not to fight them or worry about them (more water-churning) but to let them make their way to the shore. Zen, the roshi said, was fundamentally *zazen*. This was the heart of Buddhism. The way of the Buddha was to sit calmly in the purity of one's Buddha-nature, which was not something yet-to-be-attained, nor something lost and needing desperately to be found and recovered. To sit as Buddha sat is to sit in that seat where one is not tossed to and fro between happy and sad, joy and sorrow, belief and doubt, *sukha* and *dukkha* (sweet/sour, pleasant/painful), or the horns of a koan-dilemma.

"Zen, the roshi kept insisting, was not some form of excitement or ecstasy, not *sukha* (happiness) without *dukkha* (suffering), or a puzzle to be solved, but a way of living at the center of one's being. I was, then, to keep myself from excesses and extremes of all sorts, including those in the guise of religious practice and emotion. I was to 'just sit' and have faith that in this act the Buddha-nature would be manifest and would permeate all aspects of my life. In the very midst of daily activity, even of the turmoil and the up-and-down that is so much a part of life, I would learn to live at and from this center. Then I would have, as he put it, 'everyday happy-day life'.

"The cheerful, calm, constant manner of the roshi seemed to exemplify this. He radiated a quiet energy. It was said that he required only three hours of sleep nightly. Yet his teachings were at such variance with what I had read about Zen that I began to doubt the authenticity of the roshi. I had come from a fundamentalist Protestant background where considerable emphasis had been placed upon the fallenness of one's natural estate, and one's need of a thorough spiritual transformation. A Zen which used a similar scenario, though with a Buddhist cast of characters, had a familiar ring to it. Yet the Zen I now encountered seemed to run counter to this common structure of belief, Christian or Buddhist. Was this the 'real thing' or was it merely *bompu* Zen [elementary teaching in concentration]? Why did the roshi seem to avoid the issue of enlightenment, or talk about it so curiously? Could it be that he had never had the experience himself? Why was he here in America anyway, especially Chicago? I began to wonder even more when I learned that occasionally he instructed members of the Chicago police force in the martial arts.

"One day the roshi received word that his elder brother, a Zen priest, had died. Soon there was an invitation to return and take charge of the family temple. When asked why he did not return to Japan he laughed and said, 'Because I like hot, running water'. My doubts mounted. This was not, however, the 'great ball of doubt' which Rinzai teachers talk about and encourage. It was not even a doubt concerning some point of Buddhist doctrine. It was a doubt created for me by the apparent disparity between what I had read about Zen and what I was actually encountering, which seemed so different as to appear either contradictory or watered-down.

"I was still—I realized more clearly later—looking for an extraordinary experience, a kind of spiritual and psychological analog to breaking through the sound barrier or being struck by lightning. I was determined to keep climbing the mountain of zazen until IT happened: to attend every meditation session I could, to meditate in the morning and evening. Yet at the same time I was frequently taken with the feeling of how natural zazen was, even though the posture was not natural at first. The hard thing was sitting in a lotus instead of a lounging posture. How much sense it all made in a culture so busy and noisy and full of words! There was an immediate impression of truth about it, and it corresponded to things I had felt or thought before.

"Eventually a climax came, but it was not the climax or insight I had been looking for. I suddenly realized one day that I had been through this scenario once before, as a teenager—*deja vu*. Our home church, like many others in the Bible Belt, had had a week of evangelistic meetings once or twice a year. Actually almost every Sunday but Mother's Day was an evangelistic service with a sermon calculated to arouse a sense of the sinfulness of the human condition and the necessity of a spiritual rebirth and regeneration. But a whole week of evangelistic meetings intensified the mood and effect—like a week-long *sesshin*—and was more successful in bringing about a feeling of lostness and an experience of being 'born again'. For those who had already had the experience, the services also functioned as a 'revival' and deepening of one's spiritual understanding.

"I remembered what an important part of these meetings the

103

testimonial was—of the visiting evangelist, or a member of the congregation—the most memorable and effective of which began by painting, sometimes in lurid detail, the former pit of evil and suffering from which they had been saved and brought into the light. I recall how envious I was of the depths of depravity and despair into which these witnesses had fallen, which made possible such stirring anecdotes. I became sorely tempted to go off for a season and become a drug addict, engage in criminal activities, frequent places of prostitution, gamble for high stakes, and hopefully also require the services of a psychiatrist, so that I could then climb out of the abyss, have my life completely changed, and have a thrilling story of my own to tell.

"The ironic result of this was that I spent recurrent periods in misery over the failures and inadequacies of my life, not because I had sinned wickedly but because I had not been wicked enough. I despaired over not being in despair, and felt guilty for not feeling a deep sense of guilt. I had nothing to testify to but a relatively normal, ordinary, commonplace life and a collection of minor sins.

"As these remembrances flashed before me I experienced a sudden sense of relief and liberation. The Zen testimonials I had read or heard about had revived this earlier desire for being struck by the thunder-and-lightning of Mt. Sinai. And they had led me to spurn or ignore the still small voices without and within. I now realized the point of the roshi's firm but gentle guidance. I had been attempting to conform to the pattern of others whose lives and experiences were not my own. From this time on I stopped trying to throw myself into the pit or search dark recesses for dragons to battle. My Zen practice began to proceed more smoothly and naturally. And I laid to rest any further thought of waiting for the tile to fall off the roof and strike me on the head. The lotus rises from the bottom of the pond; the flower unfolds to the light."[2]

NOTES

PROLOGUE: THE MYSTIQUE OF ZEN

1. Conrad Hyers, *Zen and the Comic Spirit*, (London: Rider, 1973).
2. Harold G. Henderson, *An Introduction to Haiku* (Garden City: Doubleday, 1958), p. 169.
3. Reiho Masunaga *A Primer of Soto Zen, A Translation of Dogen's Shobogenzo Zuimonki* (Honolulu: East-West Center Press, 1971), pp. 8, 13.
4. *Shobogenzo*, Bukkyo section, trans. by Kosen Nishiyama and John Stevens, Vol. II (Tokyo: Nakayama Shobo, 1977), p. 23.
5. *Ibid.*
6. *Ibid.*, p. 60.

CHAPTER I. THE VARIETIES OF ZEN EXPERIENCE

1. Philip Kapleau, *Zen: Dawn in the West* (Garden City: Doubleday, 1979), p. 144.
2. Kosen Imakita, *Senkai-ichiran* (Tokyo, 1958), pp. 71-72.
3. Heinrich Dumoulin, *Christianity Meets Buddhism* (Lasalle, Illinois: Religious Encounter, 1974), p. 83.
4. Shunryu Suzuki, *Zen Mind, Beginner's Mind* (New York: Weatherhill, 1970); Hakayu Taizan Maezumi and Bernard Tetsugen Glassman, *The Hazy Moon of Enlightenment* and *The Way of Everyday Life* (Los Angeles: Center Publications, 1978).
5. E.g., Francis Dojun Cook, *How to Raise an Ox: Zen Practice as Taught in Zen Master Dogen's Shobogenzo* (Los Angeles: Center Publications, 1978) and *Sounds of Valley Streams* (New York: SUNY Press, 1988); Reiho Masunaga, *A Primer of Soto Zen;* and the Nishiyama/ Stevens translation of the *Shobogenzo*. Abe Masao has also been translating portions of the *Shobogenzo* in recent issues of *The Eastern Buddhist*.
6. S. Suzuki, *Zen Mind*, p. 9.
7. *Ibid.*

8. *Ibid.*, p. 28.
9. *Ibid.*, p. 135.
10. Philip Kapleau, *Three Pillars of Zen* (New York: Harper and Row, 1967), pp. 25-26.
11. *Hokyo-ki*, sec. 16-17.
12. Kapleau, *Zen: Dawn*, p. 49.
13. *Ibid.*, p. 50.
14. Daisetz T. Suzuki, *An Introduction to Zen Buddhism* (London: Rider and Company, 1949), p. 189.
15. S. Suzuki, *Zen Mind*, p. 14.
16. *Ibid.*, p. 49.
17. Kapleau, *Three Pillars*, p. 149.
18. S. Suzuki, *Zen Mind*, p. 99.
19. Kapleau, *Three Pillars*, p. 114.
20. *Ibid.*, p. 65.
21. William James, *The Varieties of Religious Experience* (New York: Longman's, Green and Co., 1902), p. 79.
22. *Ibid.*, p. 162.
23. Zenkei Shibayama, *A Flower Does Not Talk*, trans. Sumiko Kudo (Rutland, Vt.: Charles E. Tuttle Co., 1970), pp. 46-47.
24. Kapleau, *Three Pillars*, p. 228.
25. *Ibid.*, p. 229.
26. *Ten Directions* (June, 1981), p. 3.
27. Kapleau, *Three Pillars*, p. 154.
28. Trevor Leggett, *The Tiger's Cave* (London: Rider and Co., 1964), p. 37.
29. S. Suzuki, *Zen Mind*, p. 55.

CHAPTER II. BORN-AGAIN BUDDHISM: HAKUIN

1. Cited in Philip Kapleau, *Three Pillars*, p. 168.
2. Conrad Hyers, *Zen and the Comic Spirit*, p. 39.
3. Philip Yampolsky, *The Zen Master Hakuin: Selected Writings* (New York: Columbia University Press, 1971), p. 116.
4. *Ibid.*, p. 117.
5. William James, *The Varieties of Religious Experience*, lectures VI-VII.

6. *Ibid.*, lecture VIII.
7. Yampolsky, *Hakuin*, p. 118.
8. *Ibid.*
9. Winston and Jocelyn King, translators, "The Fourth Letter from Hakuin's *Orategama*," *The Eastern Buddhist*, n.s. Vol. V, no. 1 (May 1972), p. 95.
10. Yampolsky, *Hakuin*, p. 135.
11. *Ibid.*, p. 144.
12. James, *Varieties*, p. 142.
13. Yampolsky, *Hakuin*, p. 136.
14. King, *Orategama*, p. 86.
15. *Ibid.*, p. 87.
16. *Orategama* III.
17. Yampolsky, *Hakuin*, p. 25.
18. *Ibid.*, p. 133.
19. *Ibid.*, p. 146.
20. *Ibid.*, p. 91.
21. *Ibid.*, p. 94.
22. *Ibid.*, p. 119.
23. *Ibid.*, p. 118.
24. *Ibid.*
25. *Ibid.*, p. 121.
26. From Hakuin's *Yasenkanna*, quoted in Leggett, *Tiger's Cave*, p. 142.
27. *Ibid.*, pp. 142-3.
28. Yampolsky, *Hakuin*, pp. 121-2.
29. *Ibid.*, p. 66.
30. Mumon, *The Mumonkan* ("The No-Gate").
31. Yampolsky, *Hakuin*, pp. 73, 75, 82-3.
32. *Ibid.*, p. 65.
33. *Ibid.*, p. 39.
34. *Ibid.*, p. 69.
35. *Ibid.*, p. 164.
36. *Ibid.*, p. 32.
37. *Ibid.*, p. 170.
38. *Ibid.*, p. 53.
39. *Ibid.*, p. 57.
40. *Ibid.*, p. 34.

41. *Ibid.*, p. 58.

CHAPTER III. ONCE-BORN ZEN: DOGEN

1. Dogen 1242.
2. Dogen, *Zuimonki*, in Masanaga, *A Primer of Soto Zen*, p. 97.
3. Tahashi James Kodera, *Dogen's Formative Years in China: An Historical Study and Annotated Translation of the Hokyo-ki* (London: Routledge and Kegan Paul, Ltd., 1980), p. 23.
4. Hee-jin Kim, *Dogen Kigen, Mystical Realist* (Tucson: University of Arizona Press, 1975), p. 40.
5. Yuho Yokoi, *Zen Master Dogen*, (New York: Weatherhill, 1976), p. 62.
6. James, *Varieties*, p. 78.
7. Kim, *Dogen*, p. 87.
8. *Dogen zenji zenshu*, ed. Okubo Doshu, Vol. I, p. 345.
9. Nishayama/Stevens translation of the *Shobogenzo*, Vol. II. p. 117.
10. Kodera, *Formative Years*, p. 126.
11. *Ibid.*, p. 118.
12. *Ibid.*, p. 117.
13. *Ibid.*
14. *Ibid.*, pp. 129-30.
15. *Dogen zenji zenshu* I, 450.
16. *Kenzei-ki* in *Soto-shu zensho* (Tokyo: 1929-35), Vol. 17, p. 20.

CHAPTER IV. A PHILOSOPHY OF BUDDHIST CONFIRMATION

1. *Shobogenzo*, Cook trans., *How to Raise an Ox*, p. 96.
2. *Ibid.*, pp. 95, 97.
3. Taizan Maezumi, *The Hazy Moon*, p. 29.
4. James, *Varieties*, p. 165.
5. *Ibid.*, p. 89.
6. *Ibid.*, p. 99.
7. Yokoi, *Zen Master Dogen*, p. 29.
8. *Shobogenzo*, Nishiyama/Stevens trans., II, 124.

9. Daisetz T. Suzuki, *Essays in Zen Buddhism, Third Series* (London: Rider and Co., 1953), p. 45.

10. Kim, *Dogen*, p. 40.

11. Yokoi, *Zen Master Dogen*, p. 57.

12. *Ibid.*, p. 45.

13. Thomas P. Kasulis, *Zen Action, Zen Person* (Honolulu: University Press of Hawaii, 1981), p. 93.

14. *Ibid.*, p. 78.

15. *Hokyo-ki*, Kodera trans., p. 119.

16. Leggett, *Tiger's Cave*, p. 77.

17. *Shobogenzo*, Nishiyama/Stevens trans., II, 63.

18. *Shobogenzo*, Cook trans., p. 96.

19. Abe Masao, "Dogen on Buddha Nature," *The Eastern Buddhist*, n.s., Vol. IV, No. 1 (May, 1971), p. 39.

20. *Shobogenzo*, Cook trans., p. 44.

21. Yokoi, *Zen Master Dogen*, p. 46.

22. *Shobogenzo*, Nishiyama/Stevens trans., II, 55.

23. Kim, *Dogen*, p. 54

24. *Shobogenzo*, Nishiyama/Stevens trans., II, 26.

25. Yokoi, *Zen Master Dogen*, p. 46.

26. Philip Yampolsky, *The Platform Sutra of the Sixth Patriarch* (New York: Columbia University Press, 1967), p. 135.

27. Leggett, *Tiger's Cave*, p. 76.

28. Kim, *Dogen*, p. 33.

29. *Ibid.*

30. *Shobogenzo*, Nishiyama/Stevens trans., II, 29.

31. Abe, "Dogen," p. 79.

32. *Ibid.*, p. 48.

33. *Shobogenzo*, Nishiyama/Stevens trans., II, 104.

CHAPTER V. THE LOG JAM AND THE MUDDY POND

1. Abe Masao and Norman Waddell, translators, "Dogen's *Bendowa*," *The Eastern Buddhist*, n.s., Vol. IV, No. 1 (May, 1971), p. 128.

2. Yampolsky, *Zen Master Hakuin*, p. 47.

3. King, "Hakuin's *Orategama*," p. 86.

4. *Ibid.*, p. 104.

5. John C.H. Wu, *The Golden Age of Zen* (Taipei: National War College, 1967), p. 203.
6. Christmas Humphreys, *Buddhism* (London: Penguin Books, 1951), p. 184.
7. Alan W. Watts, *The Way of Zen* (New York: Pantheon Books, 1957), p. 155.
8. Kapleau, *Three Pillars*, p. 88.
9. Kapleau, *Zen Dawn*, p. 141.
10. *Ibid.*, pp. 153-4.
11. *Ibid.*, p. 141.
12. *Ibid.*, p. 153.
13. *Ibid.*, p. 162.
14. Kapleau, *Three Pillars*, pp. 145-6.
15. *Ibid.*, p. 147.
16. See Hyers, *Zen and the Comic Spirit*, pp. 129-30. Also see pp. 131 f. for other distinctions.
17. D.T. Suzuki, *Essays, Third Series*, p. 30.
18. Hyers, *Zen and the Comic Spirit*, p. 131.
19. *Ibid.*, p. 54.
20. Charles Luk, *Ch'an and Zen Teaching*, Vol. II (London: Rider and Co., 1961), p. 114.
21. Kapleau, *Three Pillars*, pp. 42-46.
22. *Ibid.*, p. 46.
23. *Ibid.*
24. *Ibid.*, p. 61.
25. *Ibid.*
26. Yokoi, *Zen Master Dogen*, p. 50.

CHAPTER VI. SOMETHING WONDERFUL, NOTHING SPECIAL

1. James, *Varieties*, p. 120.
2. *Ibid.*, p. 160.
3. *Ibid.*, p. 7.
4. *Ibid.*, p. 162.
5. Watts, *Way of Zen*, p. 170.
6. James, *Varieties*, p. 157-8.
7. *Ibid.*, p. 158.
8. *Ibid.*

9. *Ibid.*, pp. 81-2.
10. *Ibid.*, p. 87.
11. *Ibid.*, p. 79.
12. *Ibid.*, pp. 80-1.
13. Abraham Maslow, *Toward a Psychology of Being*, 2nd ed. (New York: D. Van Nostrand, 1968), pp. 71-114.
14. *Ibid.*, p. 80.
15. *Ibid.*, p. 102.
16. *Ibid.*
17. *Ibid.*, p. 80.
18. Kapleau, *Three Pillars*, pp. 287-89.
19. Shunryu Suzuki, *Zen Mind, Beginner's Mind*, pp. 57, 82.
20. *Ibid.*, pp. 58-9.
21. *Ibid.*, pp. 46, 61.
22. *Psychology Today*, August 1970, p. 16.

EPILOGUE: TWO CONTEMPORARY ZEN CASES

1. Kapleau, *Zen: Dawn*, pp. 145-51.
2. Anonymous respondent; used by permission.

INDEX